F L Y

the art of
THE CLUB FLYER

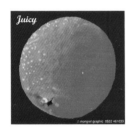

Juicy

© mongrel graphic 0532 461033

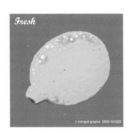

Fresh

© mongrel graphic 0532 461033

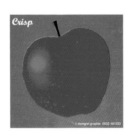

Crisp

© mongrel graphic 0532 461033

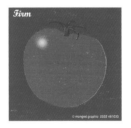

Firm

© mongrel graphic 0532 461033

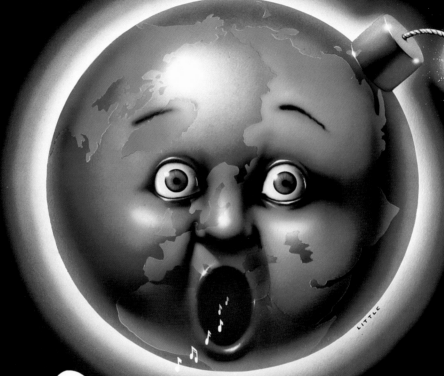

FLY

the art of
THE CLUB FLYER

nicola ackland-snow

nathan brett

steven williams

watson-guptill publications

new york

To the happy dancing nation

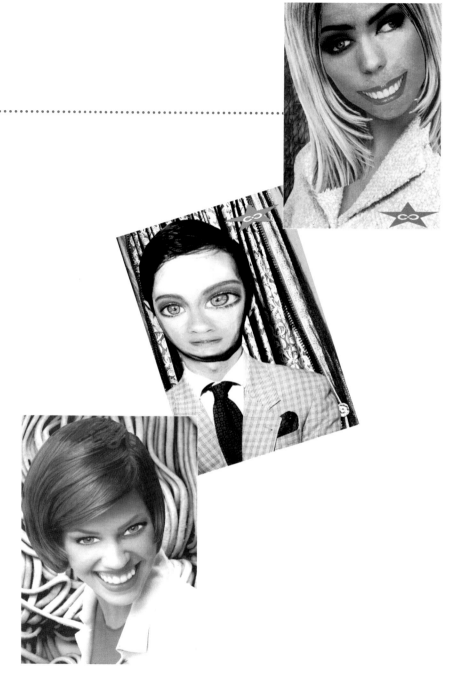

Page 1: Paul Fryer @ Mongrel Graphics; Delicious @
[Arcadia], Leeds; May 1992. Page 2: Dave Little;
[The Limelight], London; 1989 (never used)
Pages 8, 22, 36, 68 designed by Craig Richards

First published in Great Britain in 1996 by
Thames and Hudson Ltd, London

First published in the United States in 1997 by
Watson-Guptill Publications, a division of
BPI Communications, Inc., 1515 Broadway,
New York, N.Y. 10036

Library of Congress Cataloging-in-Publication Data:
Ackland-Snow, Nicola.
    Fly: the art of the club flyer / Nicola Ackland-
Snow, Nathan Brett, Steven Williams.
        p.   cm.
    "Blink."
    ISBN 0-8230-1854-7
    1. Advertising fliers—Great Britain—History—
20th century. 2. Commercial art—Great Britain
—History—20th century. 3. Graphic arts—Great
Britain—History—20th century. I. Brett, Nathan.
II. Williams, Steven, 1951– . III. Title.
NC1002.F55A34   1997
741.6'7'094109045—dc20   96-34302

Printed and bound in Hong Kong by Dai Nippon
1 2 3 4 5 / 01 00 99 98 97

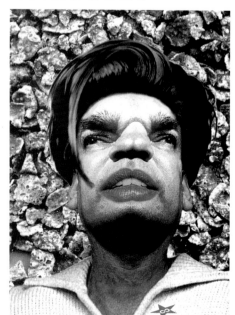

Michael Speechley; Checkpoint Charlie @ Brighton, Reading, London; 1995–96

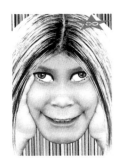

CONTENTS

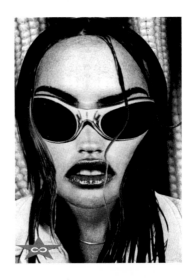

F O R E W O R D

Without those beastly bits of paper, card or plastic, I probably wouldn't be writing this – I would also probably be out of a job. In fact, our beloved clubland would be devoid of a public face, something on which to hang our reasons for dancing, loving, sharing, partying and general mayhem on a weekend.

CAMDEN PALACE

If anything, we need to be reminded that last Saturday was a corker (or an absolute wash-out!).

Where did you go, who did you see, was the DJ shite or did you believe they were the second coming! You need to kick-start the old memory bank. Rummage through those kitchen drawers (that's where the party generally ends up!). Search through your pockets. Found it! *The Flyer.*

MOVING HOUSE

This is your passport to another world, the land of a thousand dances, our reason for living. This separates you from the dole, the nine to five, those grey days. In all its forms the flyer has been with us since the Romans had chariot races. In modern times a club will not happen without the right DJ's, decor, 20k Turbo rig (sometimes!), refreshments, chill-out bar, guest DJ's from Mars, and Jeremy Healy.

For your public to know all this, it's printed on a flyer.
A mine of information, everything you need to know about your forthcoming adventure weekend. No flyer = no people = no club. They are that important. The literature of clubland, the Bible for the dance floor.

This is a book about the flyer. Have a trip down memory lane, steal a few ideas (if you're a club-runner), or just have a good read in general.

I'm off flying!

all grooved up!

Jive Turkey and Brother To Brother present

Sheffield
Every Wednesday
10-2am Occasions

funkadelicalheaven!

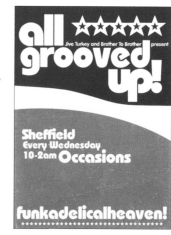

CHEESE

Ashley Beedle

Producer/Musician/DJ
(and general bod about town)

INTRODUCTION

Originating from the street and with a new instalment every week, the realms of the club flyer boast more freedom of visual expression than almost any other area of commercial art and design. The audience is youthful, receptive and eager for innovation. Usually the designer is in the auspicious position of being part of the audience (as clubber, promoter or DJ). This link provides a vehicle for him or her to stretch the imagination; what they say, we say, what we hear, they hear. As competition between clubs has increased, so has the demand for flyers and fresh design talent. As a result production levels have risen – helped by advances in Desk-Top Publishing – and black-and-white photocopies and information handbills have largely been replaced.

Whereas rock and pop music have personalities as images, dance music – in the main, and because of its electicism – lacks an obvious visual focus. Consequently, the ingredient left to the flyer to convey has been the spirit, emotion or vibe of a club. The designer must translate this into an 'image' in order to distinguish the night and entice people to go.

As clubs have become a multi-million pound industry, so the colours and icons associated with flyer design have filtered into mainstream design and onto the high street to target youth markets. However, the transience of flyers has been central to their development, together with their reflection of and reference to mainstream culture. These have enabled them to transcend fickle advertising and become collectable works of art.

This book is intended to grab and showcase the finer moments of a significant, but until recently, overlooked facet of design and youth culture. As a consequence, it also operates as a sourcebook celebrating the work of emerging designers alongside the more established names.

The flyers are organized to illustrate the elements of a club night: image, style, fun, frivolity and elation amongst many.

In the first of four chapters "Right Here, Right Now", we set the scene with a selection of flyers that refers to society, popular culture and media imagery. Heavy on irony, rebelliousness and jovial confrontation, they represent the moral and political background of club culture.

"Aphrodisia" captures the flirtation and voyeurism rife in clubs, which has developed at a time when sex has become fraught with risks. Whereas in the '60s, 'free love' encouraged the breakdown of sexual taboos, the '80s and '90s have become associated with flirtation and temptation. In recent years girls have become a regular feature on flyers. However, there is more to the girls on these pages than meets the eye. They might turn you on, but would you turn them on?!

Style is the distinguishing language of clubs, and is portrayed both lyrically and graphically in "Slanguage". Here the Applemac is king and subject: subservient yet a reinforcement to talent. Word becomes image, image becomes word.

Finally to "Trifle", to waste time frivolously, the essential art of clubbing. These flyers appeal to a sense of humour and escapism, whilst their aesthetic splendour demands applause. They, more than most, are invitation rather than advertisement and celebration rather than idiom. Fun, freedom and Philip Sallon.

While the media wait for and predict the 'next big thing', club culture and design continue to move forward and diversify, indicating that there is no 'next big thing', only a multi-faceted, ever-changing thing called Dance that, at its core, is humanistic. Behind the big business and the commercial facade, there is only tribal rhythm.

Nathan Brett

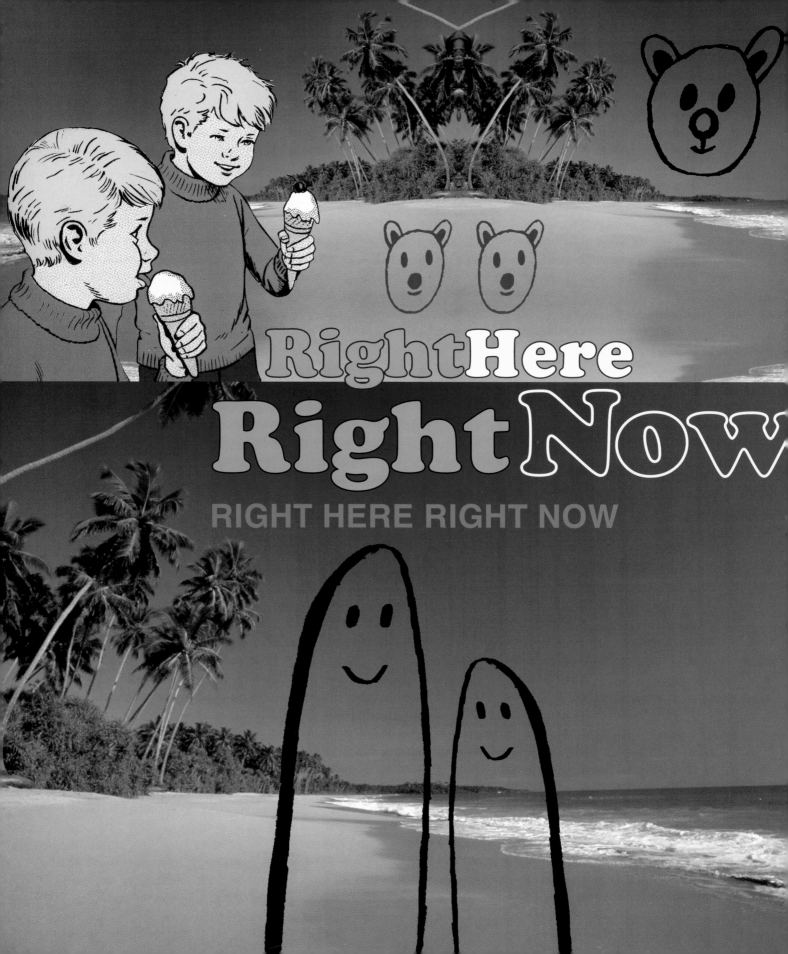

RIGHT HERE, RIGHT NOW

I was startled out of my stupor by the sound of my doorbell buzzing incessantly, a gruff voice shouted into the intercom,

"Is Dave Little there?"

"Yes," I replied, "who is it?"

"Paul Dennis" came the reply.

I had expected a visit from this larger than life character for more than a week, and here he was, stomping into the front room with a bunch of unlikely looking lads. I was introduced to them as follows: Gary Haizeman, Cymon Eckel, Terry Farley, Andy Weatherall and Steve Mayes. After lashings of tea I was informed that they needed two designs, a flyer for The Raid, and a logo and front cover for a fanzine to be called Boys Own. This was the kind of work I wanted. I was fresh out of college and working as a freelance illustrator airbrushing Twix and Silk Cut packets.

By '85 the scene had not quite gelled. Paul Oakenfold had been running Club Project in Streatham, but wanted to experiment more with a night called Future on Thursdays at the Soundshaft behind Heaven. It was an overnight success and Paul, Gary Haizeman and Ian St Paul paid me a visit to brief me on a flyer for a Monday night at Heaven to be called Spectrum.

Gary, whose favourite battle cry was by now "Acieeed!" told me, "Geordie, I want a fuck-off all-seeing eye in the middle with the words Spectrum and Heaven on Earth around it."

I guessed instantly what he wanted. I had just bought a hardback called *The Art of Rock* featuring Rick Griffin's work for the Grateful Dead which was the perfect inspiration for it. I added the words Theatre of Madness from Tom Wolfe's *Kool Aid Acid Test* and incorporated these into a Grateful Dead-style border. The reaction was fantastic – I rarely saw any discarded in the street, which was the fate of most flyers, it even ended up being exhibited at the V&A. The success and the notoriety of the club was phenomenal.

Raves began to appear across the country until the situation almost got out of hand. It felt like punk all over again, but within months the acid "downside" could be seen. Heaven and Spectrum became the focus of a media backlash spearheaded by the *Sun*. I looked in horror at kids dressed in smiley T-shirts topped off with bandannas wrapped tightly around purple, gormless faces. Cymon would scream: "Edward! Better dead than an Acid-Ted!" which became the feature headline in Boys Own exposing the demise of the acid scene.

As quickly as it started, the polarity of consciousness became fragmented once more! Again, like punk, its euphoria was as short lived as that of the drug that instigated it.

I spent most of the next year trying to kill myself on a Honda RC30 race bike I had acquired from the Isle of Man, which was much more exciting than any club/drug combination around at that time!

Boys Own channelled their energy into one-offs from Milton Keynes to Bognor.

I continued to design flyers, notably for Charlie Chester's Flying at the Comedy Store and the resurrected Raid Returns at the Limelight which was followed by Danceteria which had excellent screen-printed banners supplied by St Martin's School of Art.

By now my involvement with club graphics was waning, my relationship with promoters had turned sour. Often money owed and copyright were completely ignored, so my attention shifted to professional graphic work.

Clubs have provided me with great times and freedom to experiment with my work for which I will always be grateful, but as the old saying goes "seen it, done it, designed the t-shirt!"

Anger is an energy!

Dave Little

> **"**
> **a Haçienda flyer** does not just communicate information, but **A STYLE,** *a feeling* of what the club is about and perhaps give an idea of *the experience* to follow.
> **"**

Paul Mason:
Operations Manager
@ The Haçienda

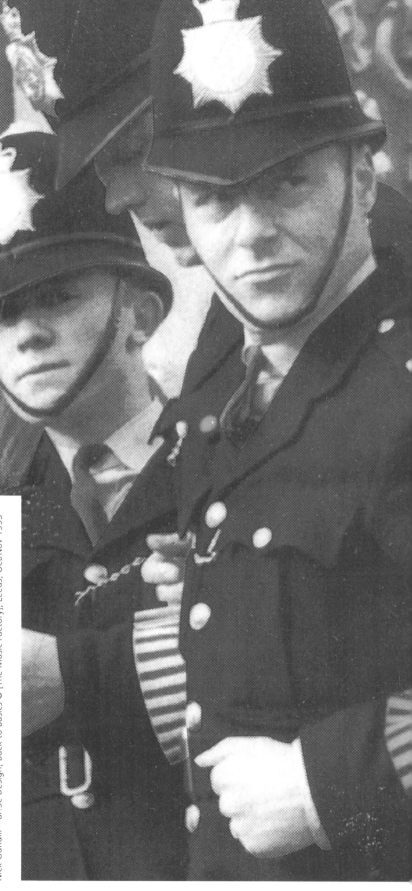

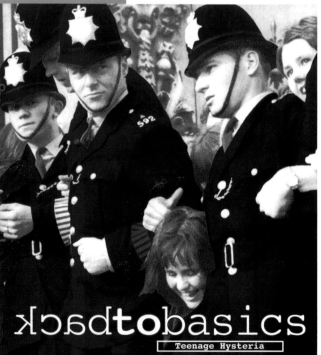

back*to*basics
Teenage Hysteria

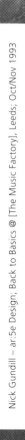

Nick Gundill – ar:5e Design; Back to Basics @ [The Music Factory], Leeds; Oct/Nov 1993

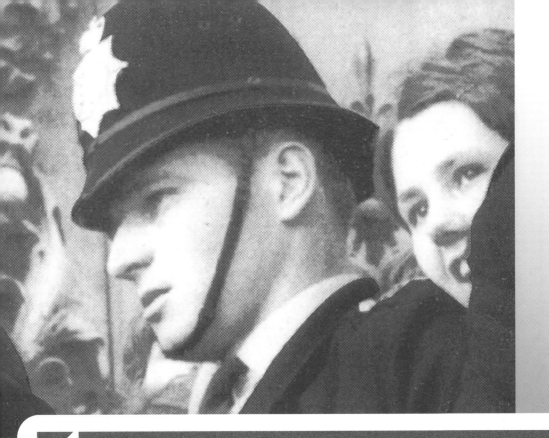

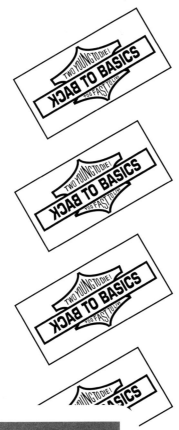

Fac 51 **The Haçienda** A MESSAGE TO ALL OUR CUSTOMERS:

As you may already know, **the Greater Manchester Police** have told us that they will be applying to revoke the **Haçienda's license** at the next magistrates meeting on the **17th of May.**

We will of course be rigorously defending the action with all our energy.

Despite our major efforts in recent months, the police feel we must do even more about removing the use of **illegal drugs** inside the Haçienda – this is where you come in – **do not,** repeat, **NOT,** buy, or take drugs in the club – and do not bring drugs onto the premises.

The prime role of your club is a place to **dance** to the most important music of the day; the only way it can continue in this way is by the complete elimination of controlled substances.

It's our club – and it's your club – we're going to **fight** to keep it alive and we expect you to be fighting with us.

PLEASE MAKE SURE EVERYONE UNDERSTANDS HOW IMPORTANT THIS MESSAGE IS. *Let's rock* – **legally.**

Directors: Anthony Wilson, Alan Erasmus, Rob Gretton, Bernard Sumner, Peter Hook, Steve Morris, Gillian Gilbert.
Management: Paul Mason, Paul Cons, Leroy Richardson.
Dj's: Mike Pickering, Graeme Park, John daSilva, Nick Arrojo, Dave Haslam.

Graham Newman; [The Haçienda], Manchester

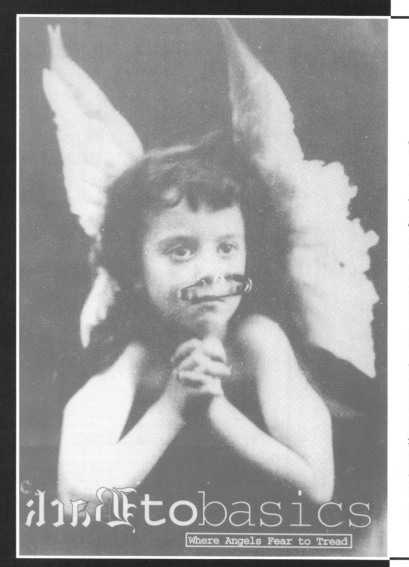

Nick Gundill – ar:5e Design; Photo Lady Margaret Cameron; Back to Basics @ [The Music Factory], Leeds; June 1993

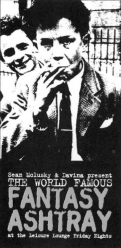

Paul Khera; Fantasy Ashtray @ [The Leisure Lounge], London; June 1994

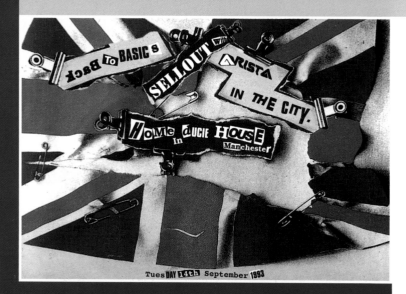

Nick Gundill – ar:5e Design; Back to Basics @ [Home], Manchester; Sept 1993

John Underwood @ FAB 4; Revolution, Revolt in Style @ [Lakota], Bristol; June/July 1995

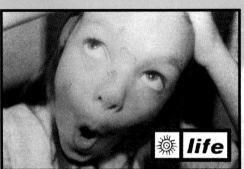

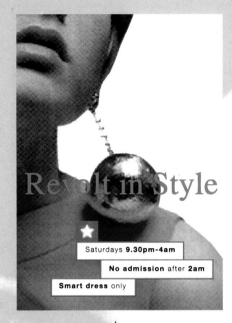

Revolt in Style

Saturdays 9.30pm-4am

No admission after 2am

Smart dress only

pull
yer face

was the name decided on for a night where
ALL HELL WAS GONNA BREAK LOOSE.

Hands up,

inhibitions down,
was to be the policy.

And the flyer had to capture the atmosphere of an

'I don't give a damn
how daft I look'
attitude.

So there I was, putting film in the camera
when my kid sister, Karen, came along.

Go on, Kaz,
pull yer face
for the camera...

and there you have it.

jeez christ, luv.

"Shave Yer Tongue.

The rebellious teenager of

acid house

with pure rock and roll **hedonism.**

A club that truly changed people's lives,

for better or for worse!

"

Martin Madigan

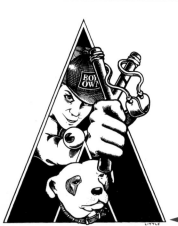

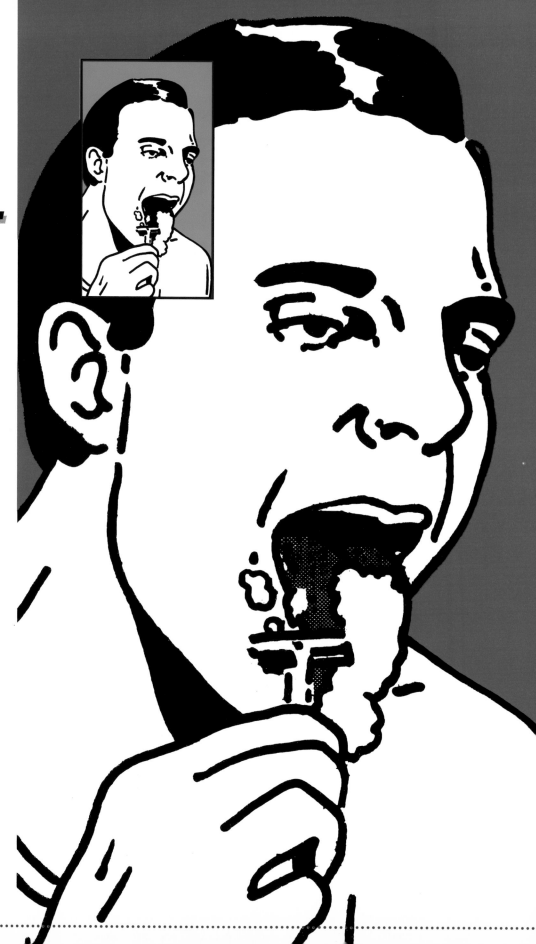

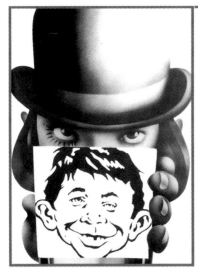

Daniel Gould; Clockwork Orange @ [Southwark Walk Studios], London; March 1994

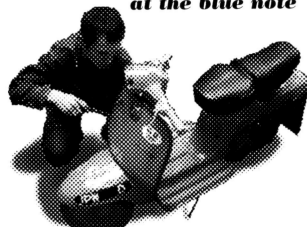

ACID JAZZ

DOIN' IT
at the blue note

with DJs
Bob Jones
Daddy Bug
Maggot

pure soul, no house,
no techno, no distractions

Saturday 17th December
10pm–5am

ADMN   £6   £4 NUS/UB40
AFTER 11   £8   £6 NUS/UB40

Miller PILSNER

THE BLUE NOTE IN ASSOCIATION WITH MILLER
1 HOXTON SQ. LONDON

Ceri Thomas – Jazz Café; Doin' it @ [The Blue Note], London; Dec 1994

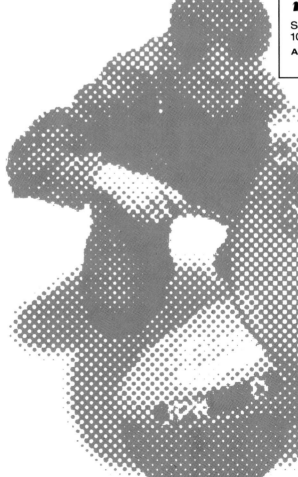

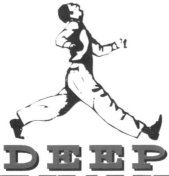

Danny De Courtelle presents
EVERY FRIDAY

DEEP FUNK

ORMANDS, 91 Jermyn Street Piccadilly, SW1
10.00pm-3.30am. £5 all nite

Dave Little; Boys Own @ a secret location

Danny De Courtelle; Deep Funk @ [Ormond's],
London; Fridays, 1995

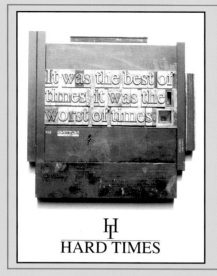

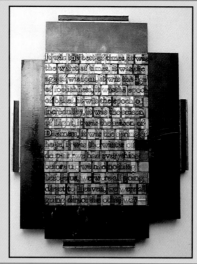

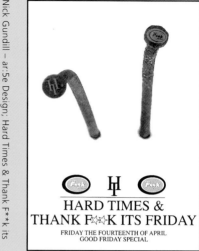

Paul Cleary (+ photo); It Was The Best of Times... @ [Hard Times], Dewsbury; Sept 1993

Nick Gundill – ar:5e Design; Hard Times & Thank F**k its Friday @ [The After Dark], Leeds; April 1995

HARD TIMES

**HARD TIMES &
THANK F☆☆K ITS FRIDAY**

FRIDAY THE FOURTEENTH OF APRIL
GOOD FRIDAY SPECIAL

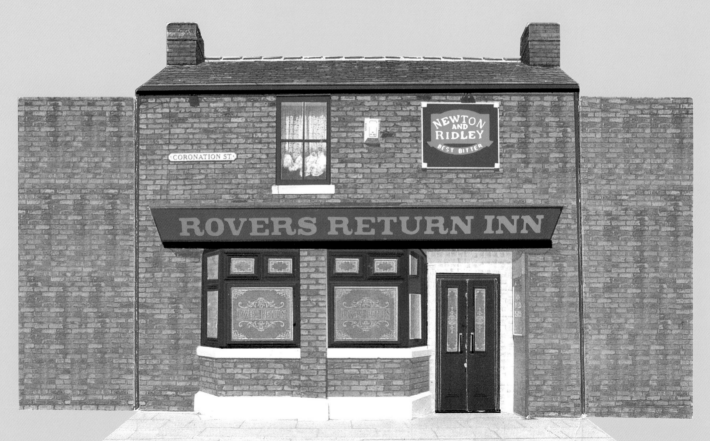

Philip Sallon; Coronation Street @ Mud Club [Bagley's Film Studios], London; Oct 1994

A flyer should be an invitation not an advert.

Paul Cleary

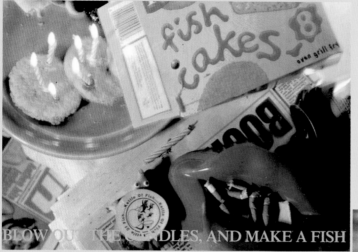

BLOW OUT THE CANDLES, AND MAKE A FISH

Kettle of Fish. Photo David Tonge; Kettle of Fish @ [Club 254], London; Dec 1995

" *We started on a* ***fishy theme*** *because they look nice in pictures and there's a fish pun for every occasion.* "

Kettle of Fish

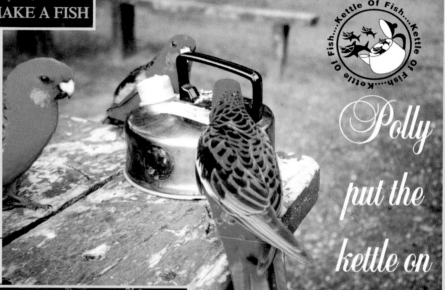

Polly put the kettle on

Kettle of Fish. Photo WIZZA DA OZ; Kettle of Fish @ [Club 254], London; March 1996

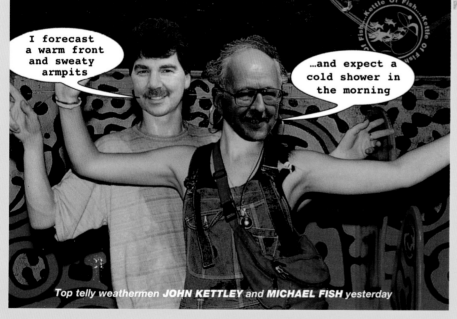

Kettle of Fish; Kettle of Fish @ [Club 254], London; July 1995

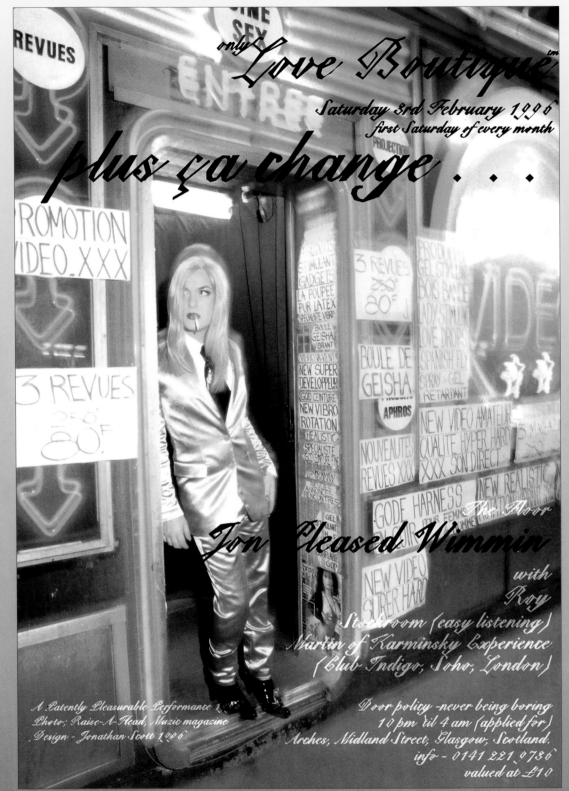

only *Love Boutique*™

Saturday 3rd February 1996
first Saturday of every month

plus ça change . . .

Jon Cleased Wimmin

The Floor

with
Roy
Stockroom (easy listening)
Martin of Karminsky Experience
(Club Indigo, Soho, London)

A Patently Pleasurable Performance 1996
Photo; Raise-A-Head, Muzic magazine
Design - Jonathan Scott 1996

Door policy -never being boring
10 pm 'til 4 am (applied for)
Arches, Midland Street, Glasgow, Scotland.
info - 0141 221 9736
valued at £10

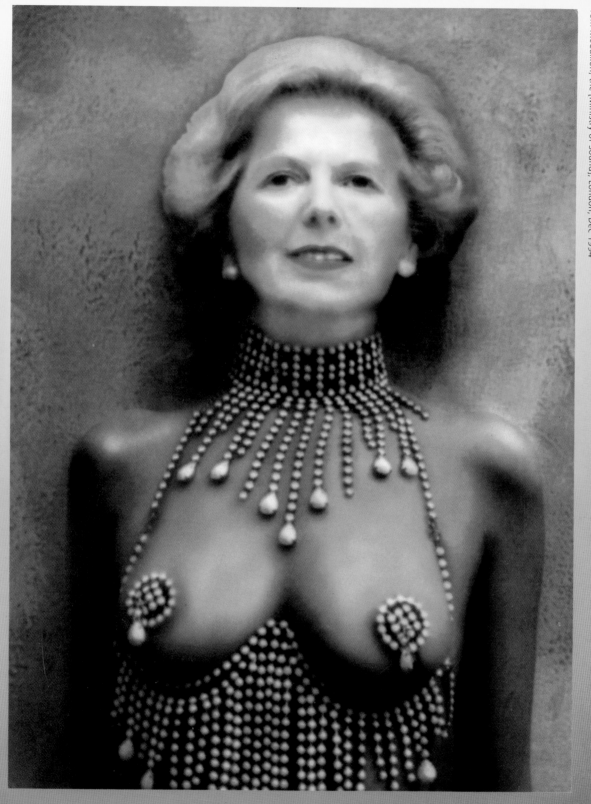

Tom McCallion; the [Ministry of Sound], London; Dec 1994

> **"** *I've seen kids pick a flyer out of the gutter, dust it down and put it in their pocket, now that's a good flyer!* **"**

Matthew Kaye

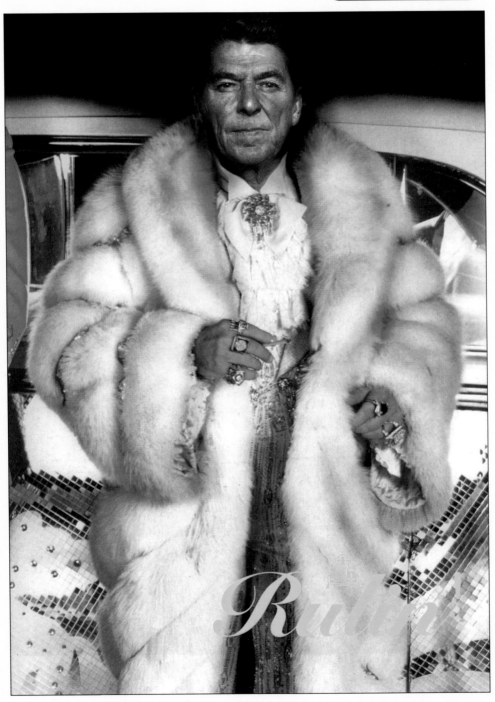

Tom McCallion; Rulin @ the [Ministry of Sound], London; Nov 1994

The KM Partnership; Starsky & Hutch
@ [Ronnie Scott's], London; Wednesdays and Thursdays 1995

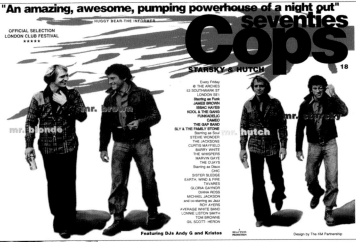

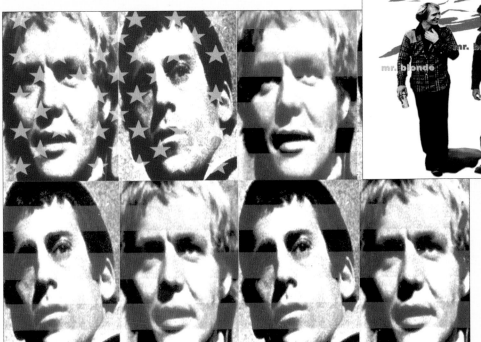

The KM Partnership; Starsky & Hutch
@ [The Arches], London; Fridays 1995

Jonathan Cutting; Glitterati @ [The Cross], London; June 1995

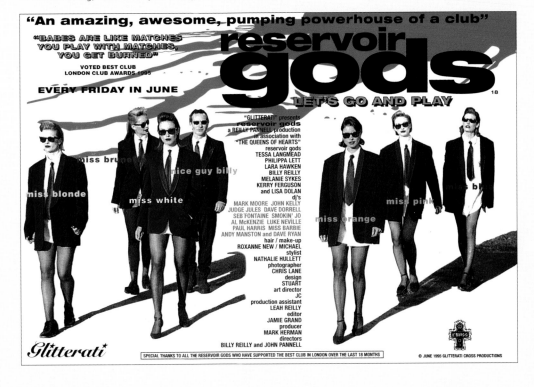

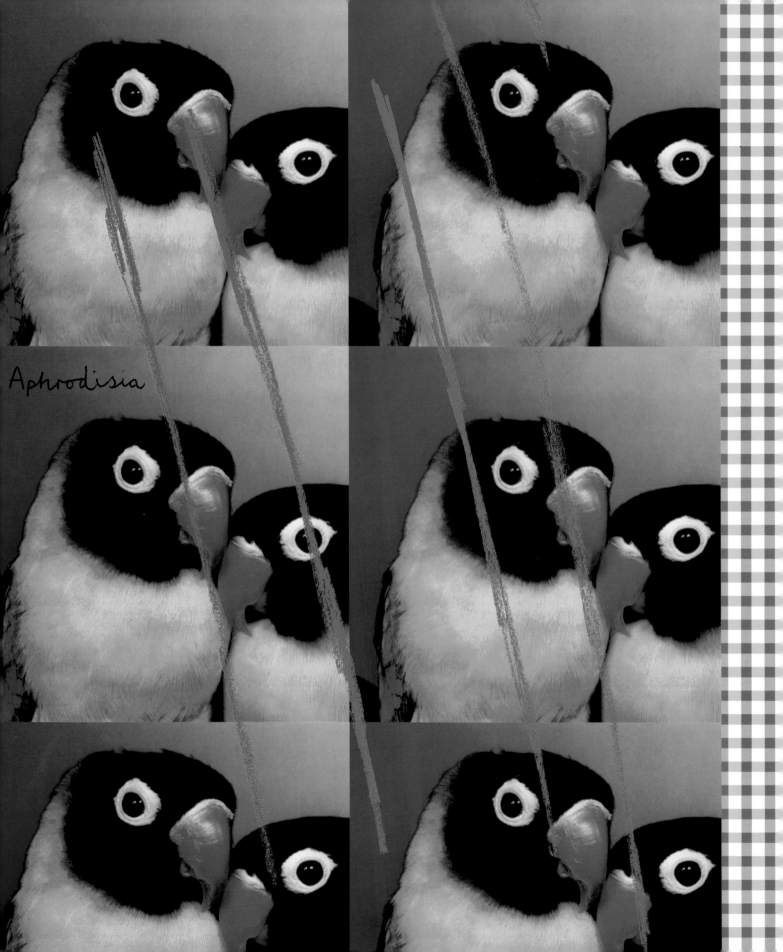

Aphrodisia

A P H R O D I S I A

Sticky Back Plastic

Sticky back plastic and elastic,
fleshtone skin-tight cat-suit,
hair scraped back away from harm,
foxes running down her arms,
and death boots –
killer cute –
her name is –
shoot –
forgotten –
nutter's daughter –
all over Pete like a bucket of water.
I'd blame it on the parent –
not a good move –
someone did – now they can't move.
But she can, in all the right places.
It's finding out where those places are
and knowing faces.

Falls off the end of the bar and shouts
"I'll fuckin' 'ave 'im".
She's trying to drown her sorrows
but they're learning how to swim.
She may seem like an obscene stream
of four-letter words – type of bird –
but keep it under your hat.
She is an extreme obscene stream
of four-letter words – type of bird
but I can see under that.
Go to kiss her mister, she'll whisper
"Don't, I'm on me own.
And that's the way I'd like to stay
until I go home."

Back to front – inside out –
a geezer in reverse –
picks herself up and screams
"MY SHOUT! I'm dying of FUCKIN' THIRST!"
You know where you heard it first.
GOOD LUCK MY SON!

Sassy Little Lassy

She's a sassy little lassy
with a classy little chassis
an' eyes on all three sides of her head.
She stumbles 'round in a micro lycra mini thing
and a back-to-back tape loop of "What She Said".
She's no mug.
She knows a fast buck takes
three to four days of renegotiations.
She'll sit in the back of a van for a week if need be,
She's

got........................

.........................PATIENCE.

Phil Dirtbox

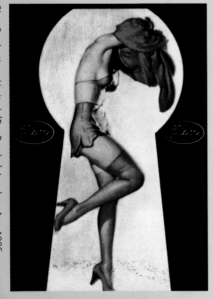

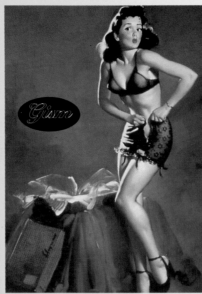

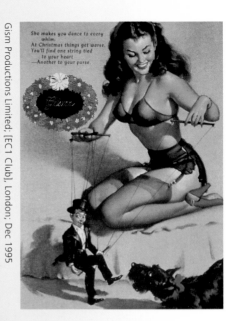

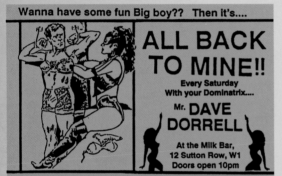

George Giorgiou; All Back to Mine @ the [Milk Bar], London; May 1992

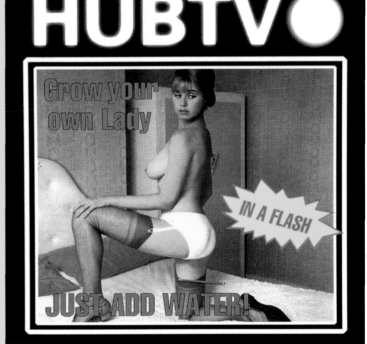

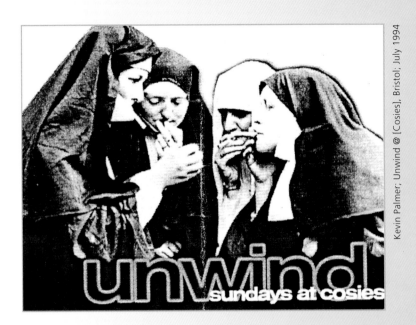

Dirtbox selection plus Ratty's Vinal Sex Pit

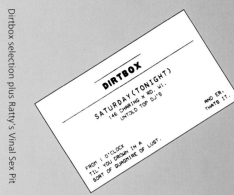

DIRTBOX

SATURDAY (TONIGHT)
146 CHARING X RD. W1.
UNTOLD TOP DJ'S

AND ER.
THATS IT.

FROM 1 O'CLOCK
'TIL YOU DROWN IN A
SORT OF QUAGMIRE OF LUST.

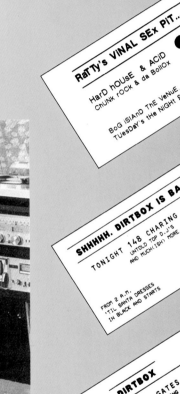

RaTTy's VINAL SEx PIT...........

HarD hOUsE & ACiD
ChUNk rOCk & da BollOx

BoG iSlAnD ThE VeNuE
TUesDaY's tHe NIGHt £1.

SHHHHH. DIRTBOX IS BACK.

TONIGHT 148 CHARING X RD.
UNTOLD TOP DJ'S
AND MUCH(ISH) MORE.

BITING CHICKS'
NECKS. THATS IT.

FROM 2 A.M.
'TIL SANTA DRESSES
IN BLACK AND STARTS

DIRTBOX

THE IRON GATES
DENMARK PLACE OFF CHARING X RD.
SATURDAY(TONIGHT BY THE WAY)

AND. ER.
THATS IT.

FROM 1 O'CLOCK
UNTIL SOMEONE
DIES OF LOVE

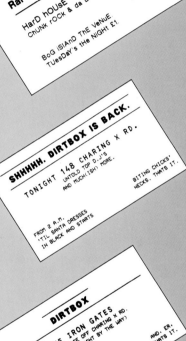

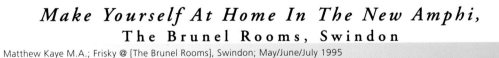

Make Yourself At Home In The New Amphi,
The Brunel Rooms, Swindon

"Knuckle-shuffling, gusset-strumming joy!"

Paddy Malone

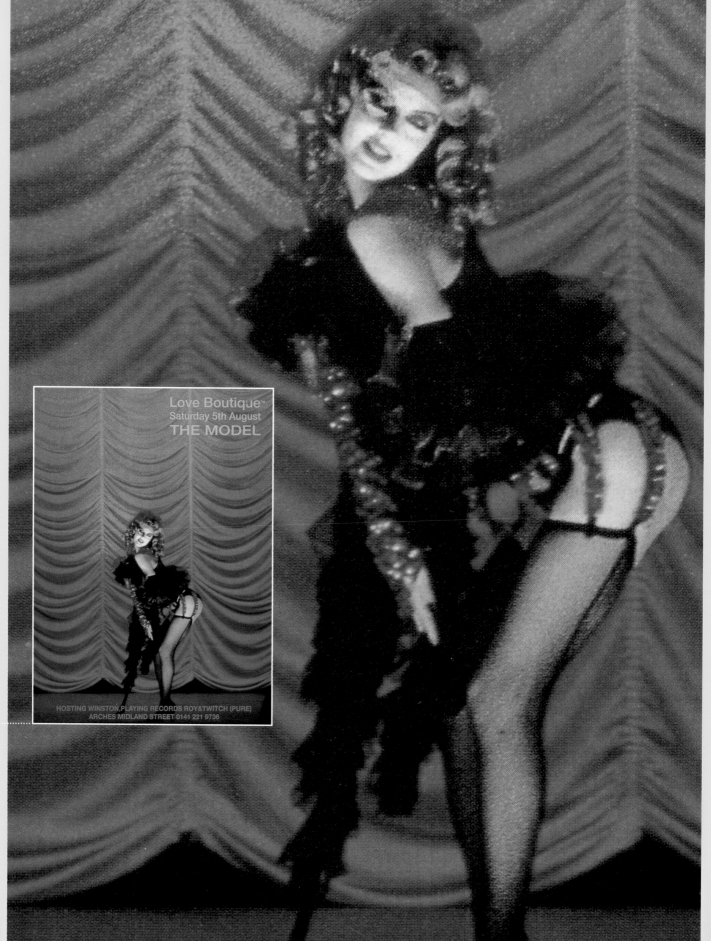

Love Boutique™
Saturday 5th August
THE MODEL

HOSTING WINSTON,PLAYING RECORDS ROY&TWITCH (PURE)
ARCHES MIDLAND STREET 0141 221 9736

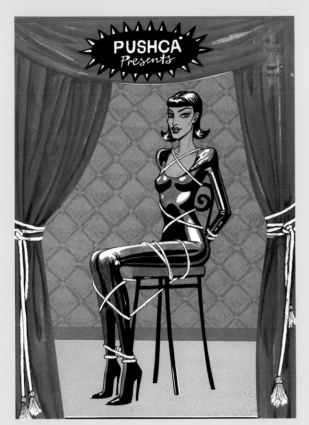

Ric and Deborah Ramswell. Illustration Jason Brooks; Pushca presents: High on Heels @ a secret London location; Oct 1994

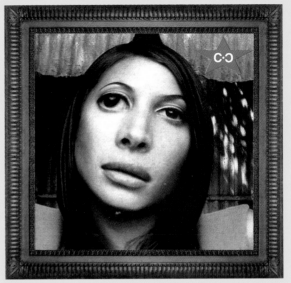

Michael Speechley; Checkpoint Charlie @ the [Showbar], Bournemouth; Nov 1995

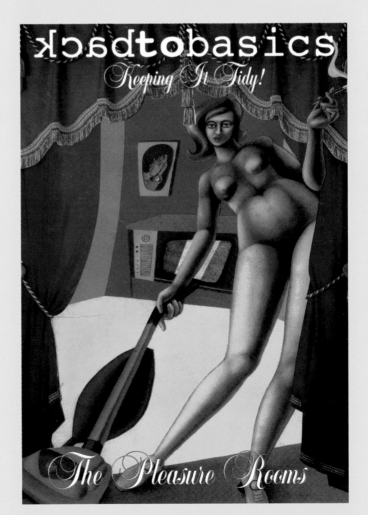

Nick Gundill – ar:5e Design. Illustration Malin Lingren; Back to Basics – Keeping it Tidy @ [The Pleasure Rooms], Leeds; May 1995

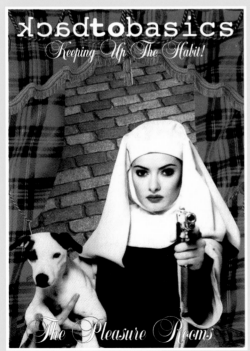

Nick Gundill – ar:5e Design; Back to Basics – Keeping up the Habit @ [The Pleasure Rooms], Leeds; June 1995

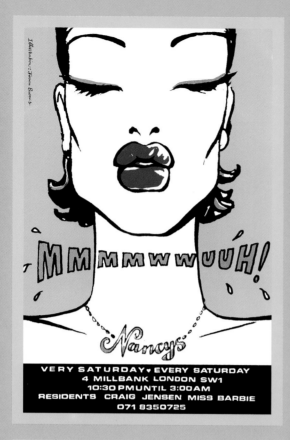

Ric and Deborah Ramswell. Illustration Jason Brooks;
Pushca presents: @ [The Atrium], London; Saturdays 1994

Ric and Deborah Ramswell. Illustration Jason Brooks; Pushca
presents: Bikini @ a secret London location; Aug 1994

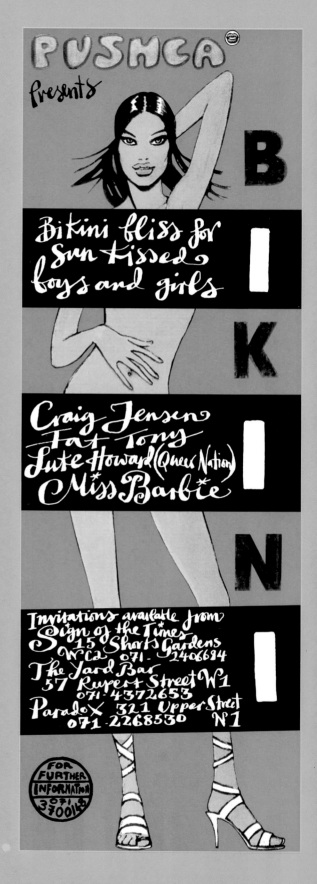

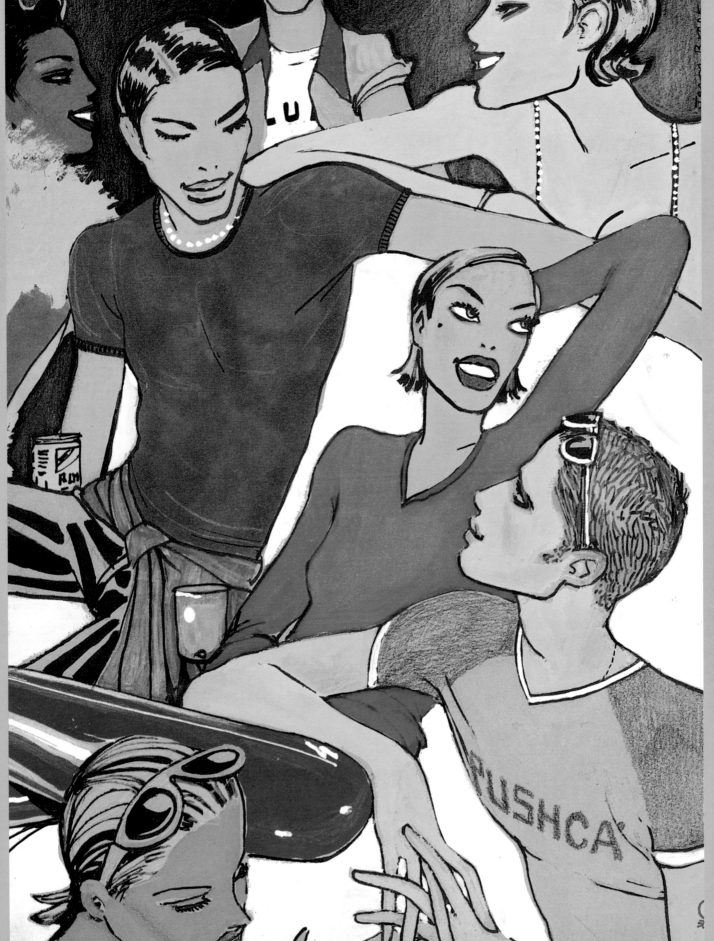

Ric and Deborah Ramswell, Illustration Jason Brooks; Pushca presents: Love to Lounge @ a secret London location; May 1995

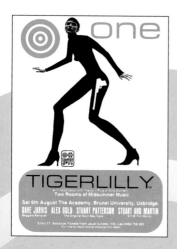

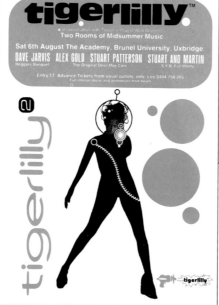

> " We wanted to have a bold and glamorous image – so I chose the name 'Tigerlilly' and developed a series of stylised photo-illustrations showing a strong female figure who resembled characters from an early 'Bond film' or Barbarella style sci-fi adventure. Tigerlilly then became our imaginary mascot who would appear in different guises on all our flyers developing her own beautiful and dangerous image. "

Leo Elstob

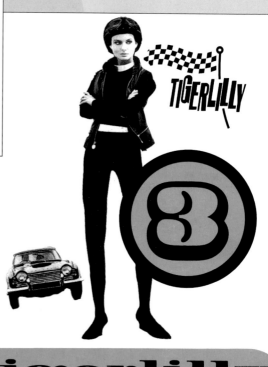

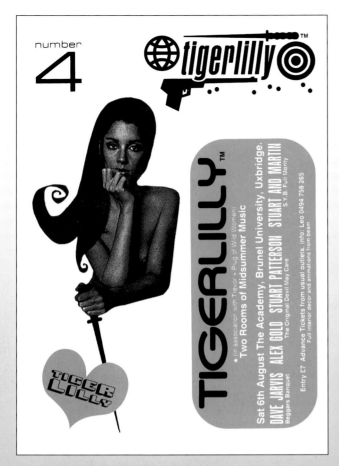

number **4**

tigerlilly™

TIGERLILLY™

* (in association with Trevor + Plug of Wild Women)
Two Rooms of Midsummer Music

Sat 6th August The Academy, Brunel University, Uxbridge.

DAVE JARVIS   ALEX GOLD   STUART PATTERSON   STUART AND MARTIN

Beggars Banquet   The Original Devil May Care   S.Y.B Full Monty

Entry £7   Advance Tickets from usual outlets, info: Leo 0494 758 265
Full interior decor and animations from beam

Leo Elstob – Bushfire Design; (X4) Tigerlilly @ [The Academy], Uxbridge; Aug 1994

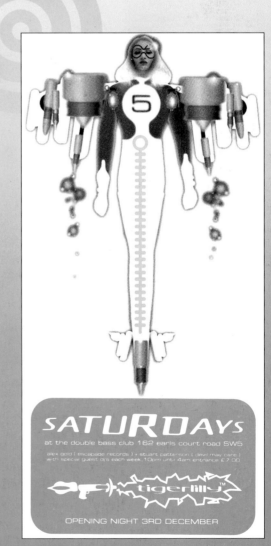

SATURDAYS

at the double bass club 162 earls court road SW5

alex gold [escapade records] + stuart patterson [devil may care]
with special guest dj's each week. 10pm until 4am entrance £7.00

tigerlilly™

OPENING NIGHT 3RD DECEMBER

Leo Elstob – Bushfire Design; Tigerlilly @ the [Double Bass Club], London; Dec 1994

"**The Tigerlilly flyers** were probably my most well received work as they managed to use just the right style of imagery for the market in 94 – preceding the explosion of tacky 'babe' flyers that hit the streets as CLUBLAND WENT GLAM CRAZY."

Leo Elstob

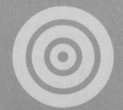

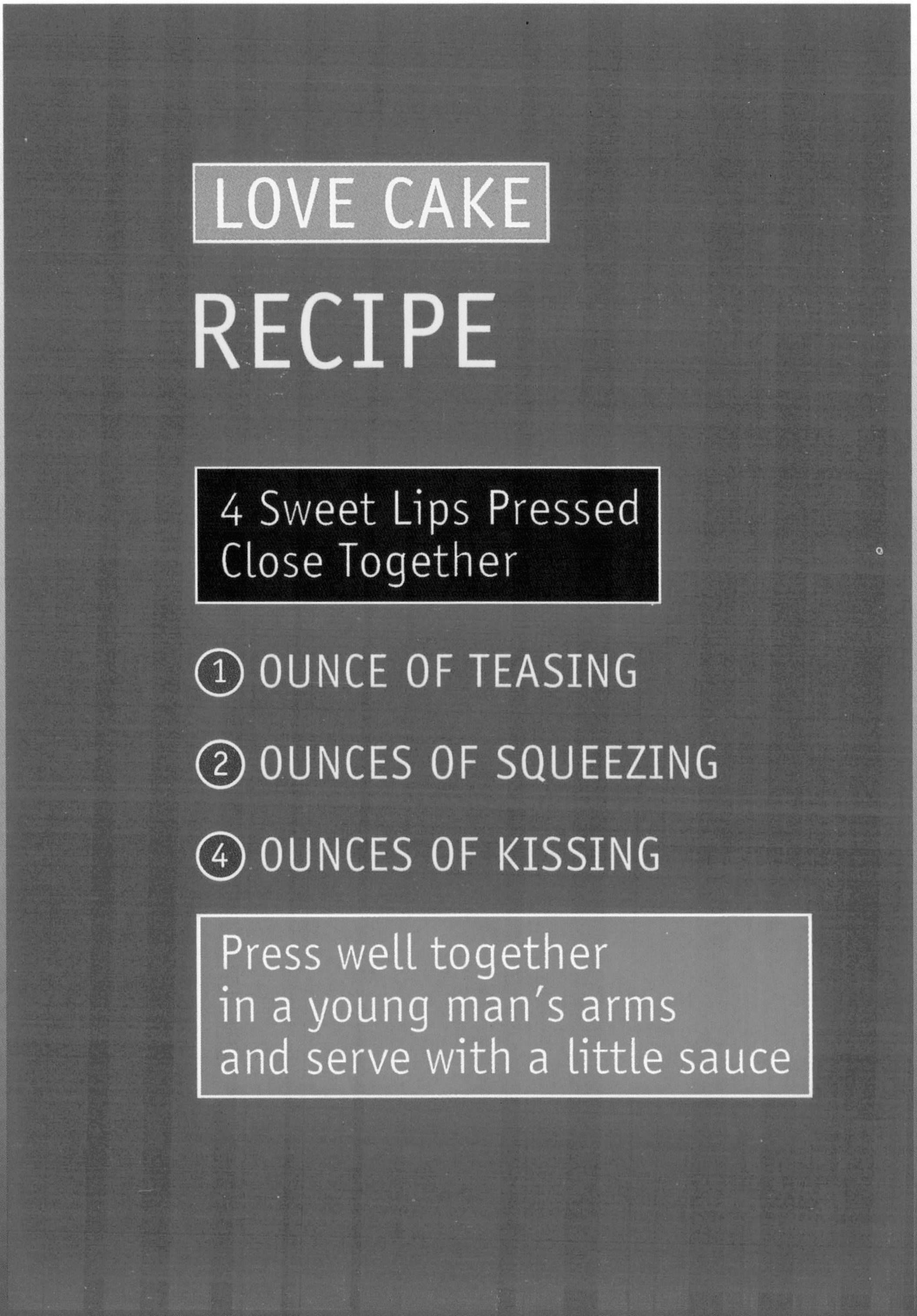

LOVE CAKE

RECIPE

4 Sweet Lips Pressed Close Together

① OUNCE OF TEASING

② OUNCES OF SQUEEZING

④ OUNCES OF KISSING

Press well together
in a young man's arms
and serve with a little sauce

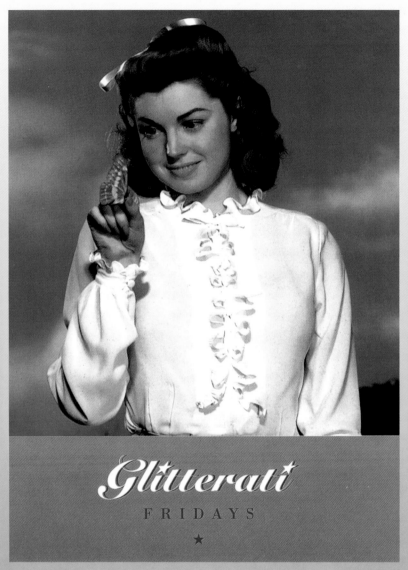

Glitterati

F R I D A Y S

★

Jonathan Cutting; Glitterati @ [The Cross], London; April 1995

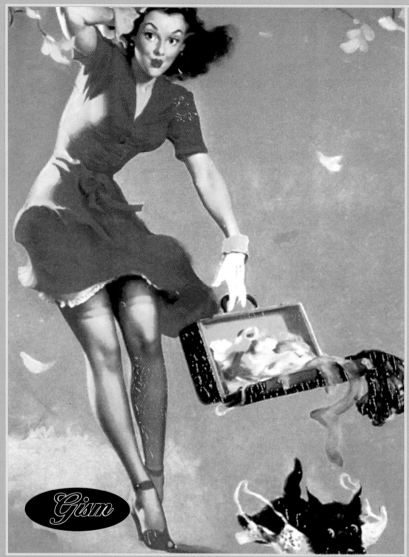
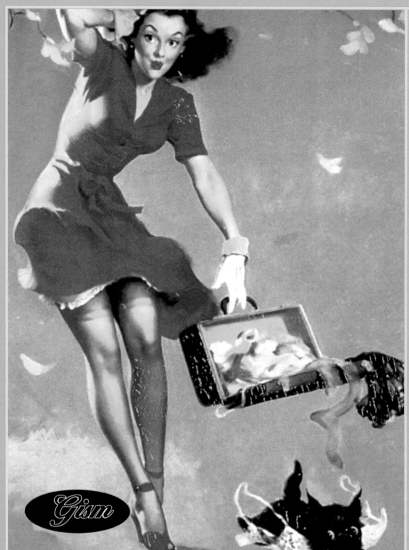

Gism Productions Limited; [Bar Rumba], London; March 1995

Billion Dollar Babes; Billion Dollar Babes @ [Raw], London; April 1994

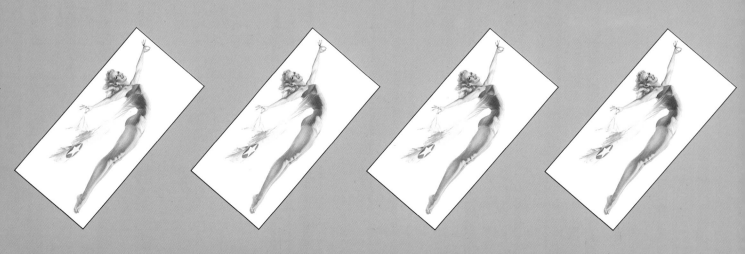

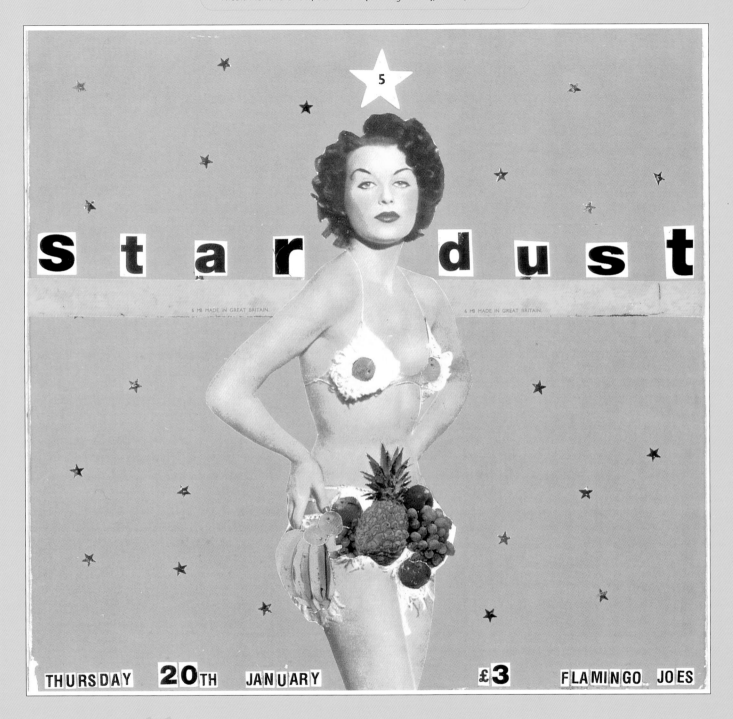

"*Doing flyers has definitely made me more attractive to the opposite sex.*"

Danny Jenkins

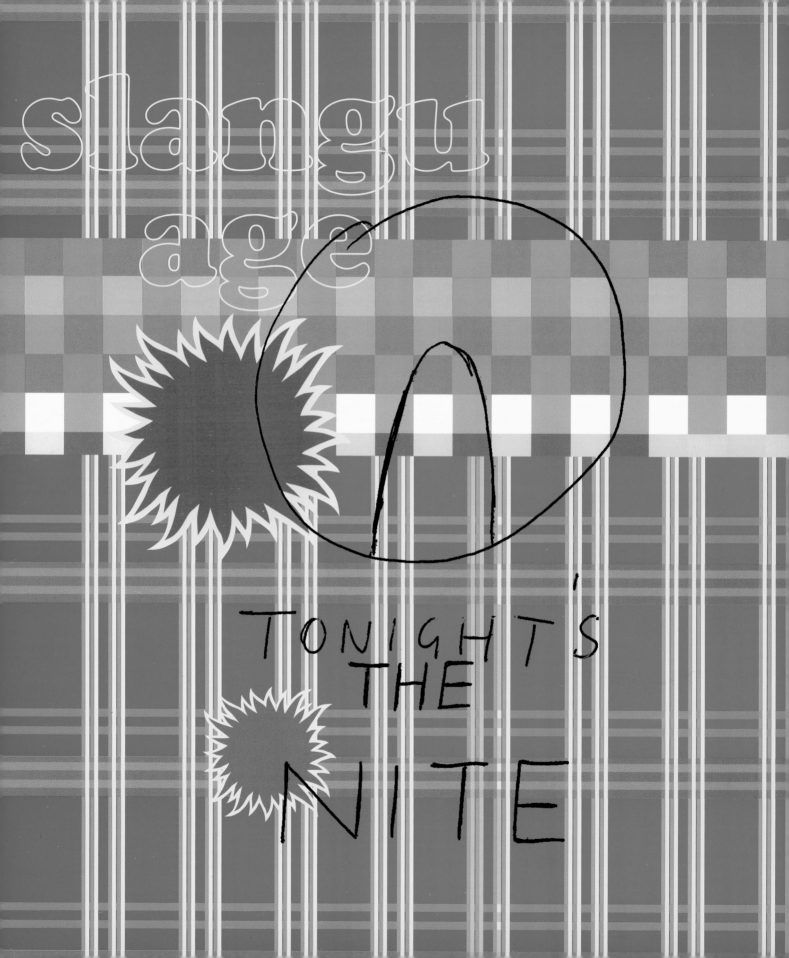

SLANGUAGE

When noise levels become too high, we have to shout to make ourselves heard.

In a visual environment, where the volume of messages we are exposed to is chaotic, we have to stop and think before we react in order to be seen amidst the crowd – to get ahead of the traffic. Audiences become quickly attuned to various styles and language, so new forms have to be applied, but as extensions not replacements.

As the majority of work in this section shows, the reduction of a message to a single word, symbol or phrase is part of a reactioning process – not usually because those flyers are trying to act as statements, but more often simply because they look good visually. They begin to form a new language that plays a game, and pokes fun at the establishment.

All of us are influenced in some way by the whole concept of multi-nationals and corporate symbols – they are an integral part of our environment and social fabric. People now respond and react to brand names and logos – Coca Cola no longer needs to say Coke, its symbol has become a recognizable image in any culture. When logos are adapted or reinvented, a similar purpose is served.

Proof of how rich this visual sampling can be is particularly evident in the work of such people as the Designers Republic, who experiment by hijacking and sampling existing icons, which are then in turn re-used and remixed. There is an interesting parallel to be drawn with the music, which becomes an extension of the same working process, a process that has been fuelled by new technology.

Mac-culture has enabled us as designers to produce our work more quickly and with greater ease than ever before – anyone who has access to the right equipment has a facility to produce artwork. In the short term this means there will be more do-it-yourselfers producing a greater amount of work that is both bad design and uninteresting, but in a wider sense it means more intuitive people can harness this media to push and develop new ideas and working methods.

Flyers themselves have always been very much a disposable item because of the time-frame they operate within, and for this reason they can function as vehicles that become very immediate outlets for creativity and expression – a kind of spontaneous testing ground where visual experiments can be tried and rejected. Every flyer is therefore unique in that it maps a certain period of style or fashion, and forms an entertaining statement of its own particular place or time. The beauty of this medium is that you are completely free of any corporate constraint – an asset that should be both enjoyed and exploited.

Tom Hingston

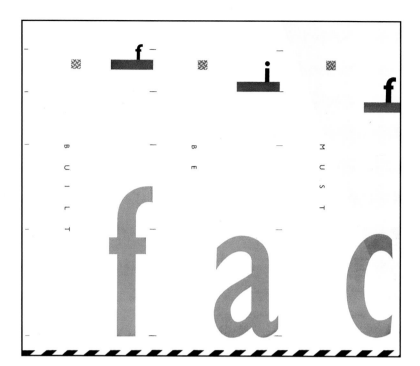

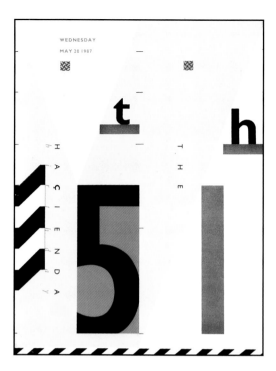

Trevor Johnson; 5th Birthday @ [the Haçienda], Manchester; May 1987

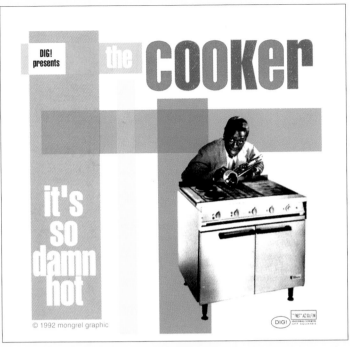

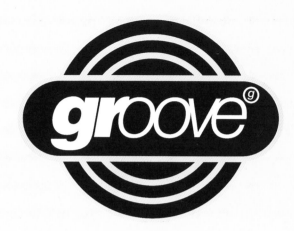

Paul Fryer @ Mongrel Graphics; The Cooker @ [Arcadia], Leeds; 1992

Steve Swindells @ Groove launch party @ [Emporium], London, May 1988

'Groove'

grew out of the original

'Downbeat' jam sessions
(Piano bar '85, Frith St.
and Brown's,
Thursdays, '88 and '89).

The format has been much emulated
but

'Downbeat'

was the 1st!

Steve Swindells

Paul Fryer @ Mongrel Graphics; Joy @ the [Warehouse], Leeds; June 1991

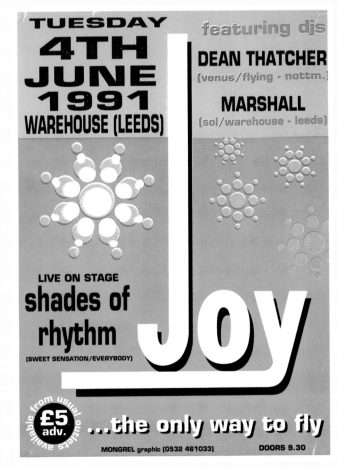

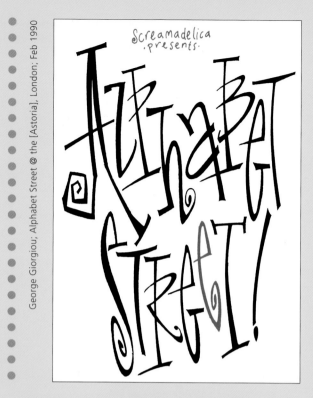

Danny Rampling and George Giorgiou; Shoom @ [Crown House], London; Jan 1993

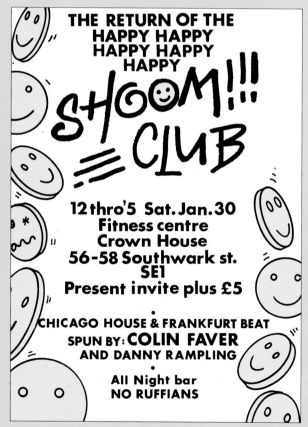

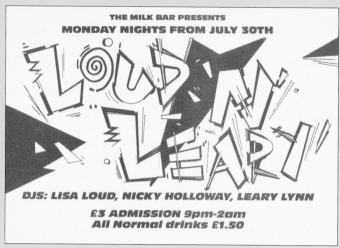

George Giorgiou; Loud 'n' Leary @ [The Milk Bar], London; July 1990

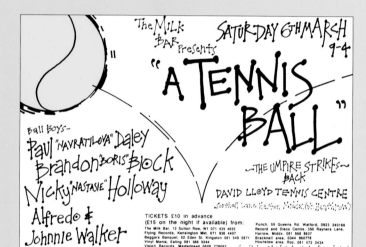

George Giorgiou; A Tennis Ball @ the [David Lloyd Tennis Club], Middlesex; March 1993

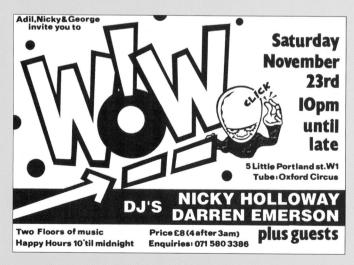

George Giorgiou; Wow @ a London venue; Nov 1991

Dave Little; Future @ [The Soundshaft], London; 1988

Dave Little;
Qué Pasa @
a secret location,
London; 1993

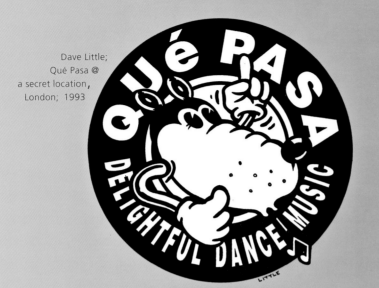

Dave Little; Boys Own @ a secret location, London; 1988

Dave Little; The Raid @ [100 Club], London; 1985

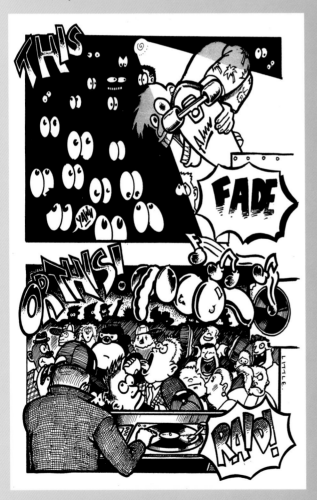

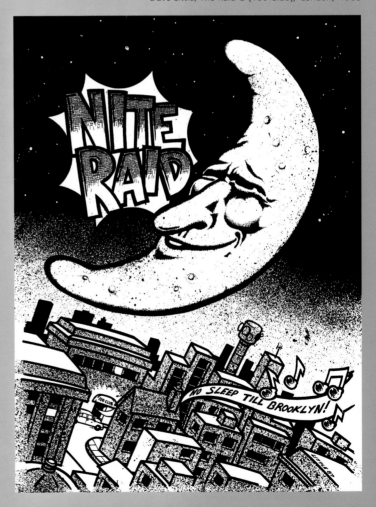

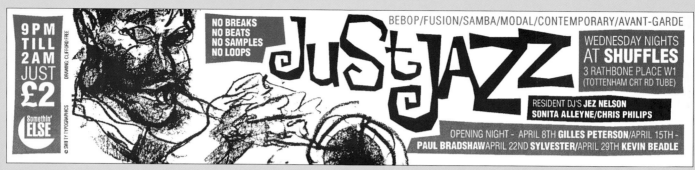

Swifty Typografix. Illustration by Clifford Free; Just Jazz @ [Shuffles], London; April 1992

> The whole thing about flyer art is its cottage industry; pockets of DJ's and designers getting together...
> For designers it's a phase to go through to get your name out there. A chance to do design work quickly.

Swifty Typografix

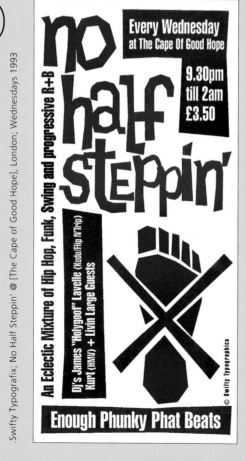

Swifty Typografix; No Half Steppin' @ [The Cape of Good Hope], London; Wednesdays 1993

Swifty Typografix; Club Red @ [Jazz Cafe], London; Sundays April 1992

Saturday 10th July '93 / 10.30PM TILL 4AM-ISH / £6.00

GIDDY-ITUS

AT CSAR RICARDO, 9 YOUNG ST, KENSINGTON W8 / BETWEEN KENSINGTON MRKT & BARKERS STORE

DJ'S: GILLES PETERSON/PATRICK FORGE/KEVIN BEADLE/MAX BEESLEY/DJ BROWNSWOOD

Swifty Typografix; Giddy-Itus @ [Csar Ricardo], London; July 1993

THURSDAYS AT THE COMEDY CAFE RIVINGTON ST EC2

DJ'S DAVE HUCKER /COLM CARTY

GRIS

£5
£3 CONC
£2 WITH FLYER

GRIS

8.30PM TILL LATE

A GLOBAL SHIMMY N' SHAKE

Swifty Typografix; Gris Gris @ the [Comedy Cafe], London; Thursdays 1993

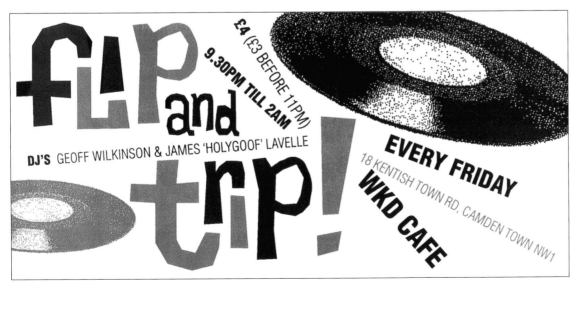

flip and trip!

£4 (£3 BEFORE 11PM)
9.30PM TILL 2AM

DJ'S GEOFF WILKINSON & JAMES 'HOLYGOOF' LAVELLE

EVERY FRIDAY
18 KENTISH TOWN RD, CAMDEN TOWN NW1

WKD CAFE

Swifty Typografix; Flip and Trip! @ the [WKD Cafe], London; March 1992

friday 17th april 10pm-5am | dj's norman jay/bro marco/femi

Shake & fingerpop

92

+ good times

£10

shake and fingerpop productions present

"the long good friday" at villa stephano next to holborn tube

Swifty Typografix; Shake & Fingerpop @ [Villa Stefano], London; April 1992

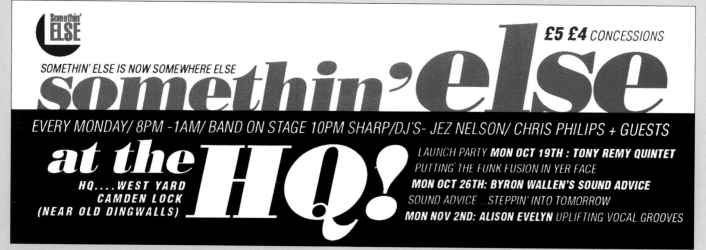

SOMETHIN' ELSE IS NOW SOMEWHERE ELSE

somethin' else

£5 £4 CONCESSIONS

EVERY MONDAY/ 8PM -1AM/ BAND ON STAGE 10PM SHARP/DJ'S- JEZ NELSON/ CHRIS PHILIPS + GUESTS

at the HQ!

HQ....WEST YARD
CAMDEN LOCK
(NEAR OLD DINGWALLS)

LAUNCH PARTY **MON OCT 19TH** : TONY REMY QUINTET
PUTTING THE FUNK FUSION IN YER FACE
MON OCT 26TH: BYRON WALLEN'S SOUND ADVICE
SOUND ADVICE....STEPPIN' INTO TOMORROW
MON NOV 2ND: ALISON EVELYN UPLIFTING VOCAL GROOVES

Swifty Typografix; Somethin' Else @ [HQ], London; Oct/Nov 1992

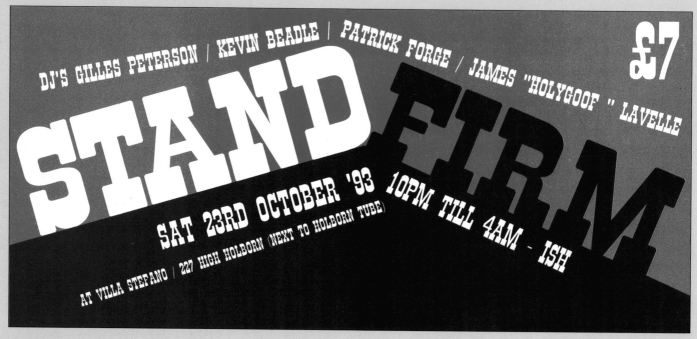

DJ'S GILLES PETERSON / KEVIN BEADLE | PATRICK FORGE / JAMES "HOLYGOOF " LAVELLE

£7

STAND FIRM

SAT 23RD OCTOBER '93 10PM TILL 4AM - ISH

AT VILLA STEFANO | 227 HIGH HOLBORN (NEXT TO HOLBORN TUBE)

Swifty Typografix; Stand Firm @ [Villa Stefano], London; Oct 1993

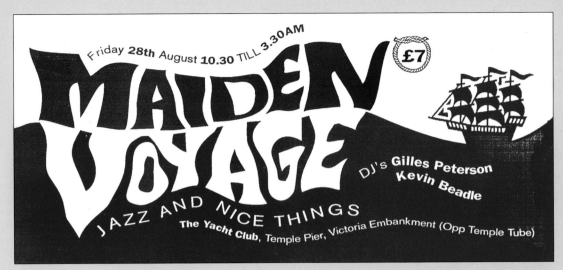

Friday 28th August 10.30 TILL 3.30AM £7

MAIDEN VOYAGE

JAZZ AND NICE THINGS

DJ's Gilles Peterson
Kevin Beadle

The Yacht Club, Temple Pier, Victoria Embankment (Opp Temple Tube)

Swifty Typografix; Maiden Voyage @ [The Yacht Club], London; Aug 1992

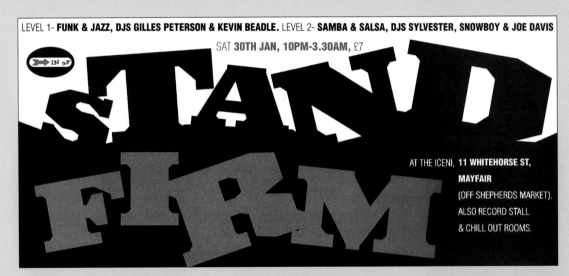

LEVEL 1- FUNK & JAZZ, DJS GILLES PETERSON & KEVIN BEADLE. LEVEL 2- SAMBA & SALSA, DJS SYLVESTER, SNOWBOY & JOE DAVIS

SAT 30TH JAN, 10PM-3.30AM, £7

IN 93'

STAND FIRM

AT THE ICENI, 11 WHITEHORSE ST, MAYFAIR
(OFF SHEPHERDS MARKET).
ALSO RECORD STALL
& CHILL OUT ROOMS.

Swifty Typografix; Stand Firm @ [The Iceni], London; Jan 1993

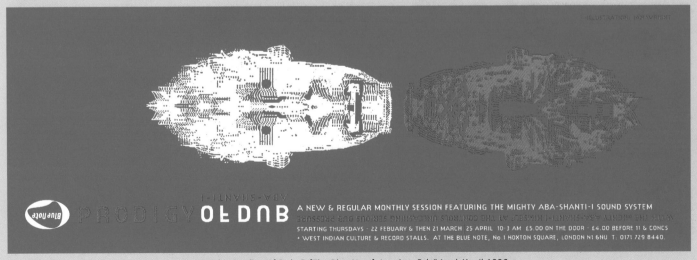

ILLUSTRATION: IAN WRIGHT

ABA-SHANTI-I
Blue Note PRODIGY OF DUB

A NEW & REGULAR MONTHLY SESSION FEATURING THE MIGHTY ABA-SHANTI-I SOUND SYSTEM
STARTING THURSDAYS · 22 FEBUARY & THEN 21 MARCH. 25 APRIL 10-3 AM £5.00 ON THE DOOR · £4.00 BEFORE 11 & CONCS
• WEST INDIAN CULTURE & RECORD STALLS. AT THE BLUE NOTE, No 1 HOXTON SQUARE, LONDON N1 6NU T. 0171 729 8440.

Tom Hingston and Paul Allen. Illustration Ian Wright; Prodigy of Dub @ [The Blue Note], London; Feb/March/April 1996

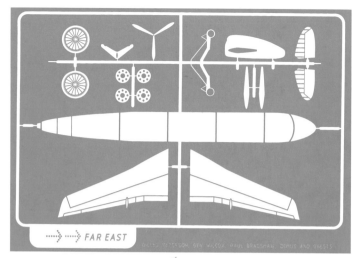

Tom Hingston and Paul Allen; Far East @ [The Blue Note], London; Dec 1995

Neil Harston and Darren Turner @ Squarepeg Design; [Golden], Manchester; Nov/Dec 1995

Tom Hingston and Paul Allen; Dig Deep @ [The Blue Note], London; Jan 1996

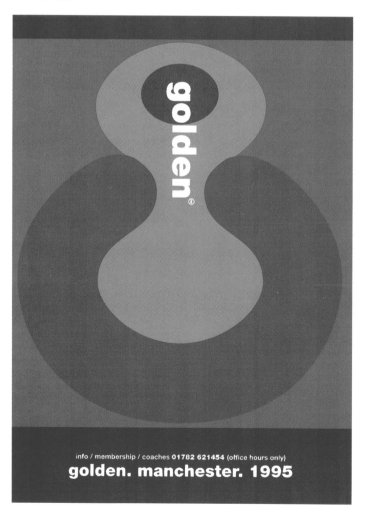

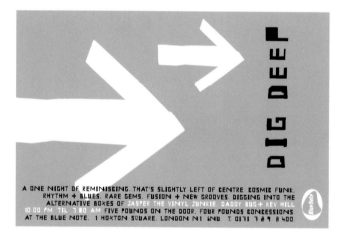

ROCK AND ROLL
DIED IN 1987.
Long live Golden!

Jon Hill — Golden Promoter

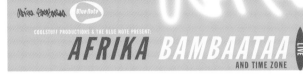

9 FEBRUARY '96 £7.00 IN ADVANCE. DOORS: 7PM ON STAGE: 9PM SHARP

COOLSTUFF PRODUCTIONS & THE BLUE NOTE PRESENT:

AFRIKA BAMBAATAA
AND TIME ZONE
LIVE

THE GODFATHER OF HIP-HOP & RENEGADE OF FUNK HITS THE BLUE NOTE FOR HIS ONLY DATE IN LONDON.
COME & TASTE THE BEST GOOD TIME, OLD SKOOL ATMOSPHERE THAT ONLY BAMBAATAA & HIS TWO DECADES ON THE MIC CAN PROVIDE, TOGETHER WITH TIME ZONE IN THE GROOVE BESIDE HIM. THE BIG MAN IS BACK. PLUS DJ PATRICK COLDSWEAT. AT THE BLUE NOTE No. 1 HOXTON SQUARE, LONDON N1 6NU. TELEPHONE 0171 729 8440 XTRA £3.00 ON THE DOOR PAYS ENTRY TO MAGIC BUS 'TILL FIVE AM. TICKETMASTER 0171 344 4444

Tom Hingston and Paul Allen; Afrika Bambaataa @ [The Blue Note], London; Feb 1996

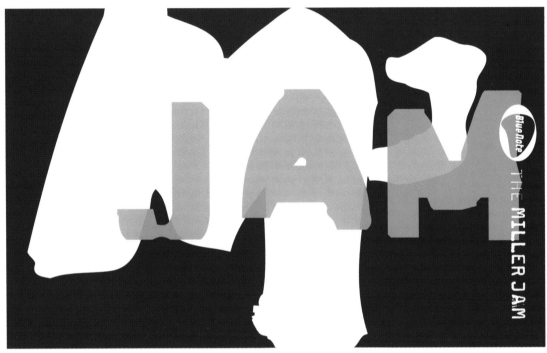

Tom Hingston and Paul Allen; Jam @ [The Blue Note], London; Wednesdays 1996

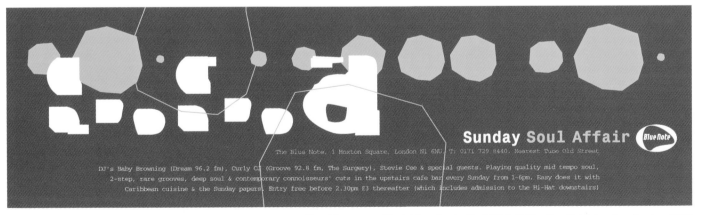

Sunday Soul Affair

The Blue Note, 1 Hoxton Square, London N1 6NU. T: 0171 729 8440. Nearest Tube Old Street

DJ's Baby Browning (Dream 96.2 fm), Curly CJ (Groove 92.8 fm, The Surgery), Stevie Cee & special guests. Playing quality mid tempo soul,
2-step, rare grooves, deep soul & contemporary connoisseurs' cuts in the upstairs cafe bar every Sunday from 1-6pm. Easy does it with
Caribbean cuisine & the Sunday papers. Entry free before 2.30pm £3 thereafter (which includes admission to the Hi-Hat downstairs)

Tom Hingston and Paul Allen; Sunday Soul Affair @ [The Blue Note], London; Sundays 1996

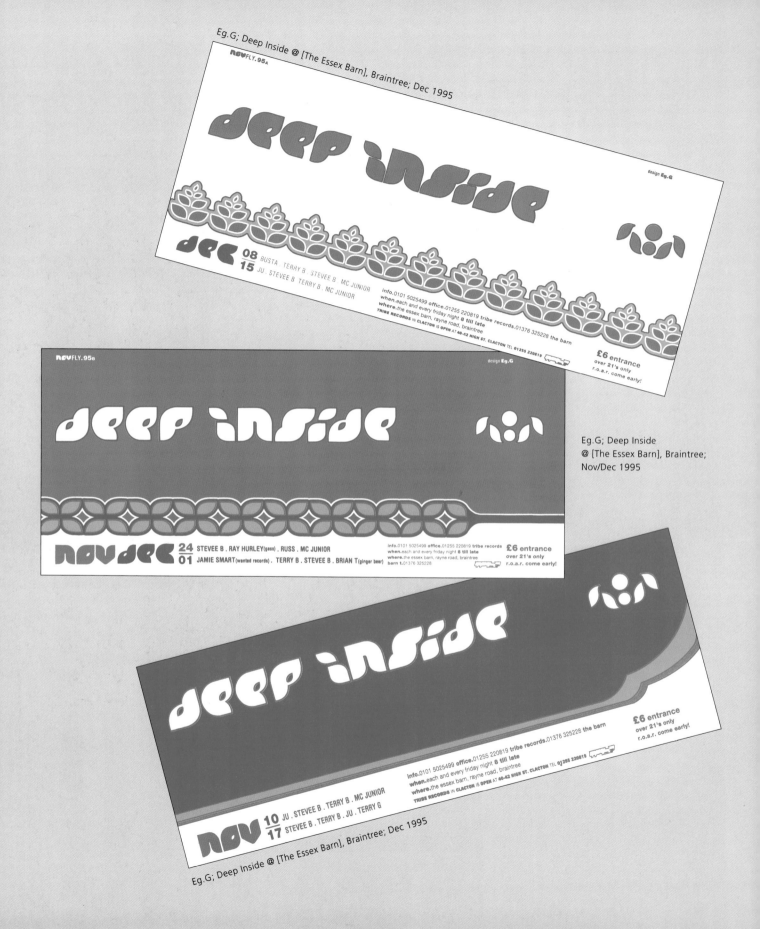

Eg.G; Deep Inside @ [The Essex Barn], Braintree; Dec 1995

novFLY.95a

deep inside

design Eg.G

DEC
08 BUSTA . TERRY B . STEVEE B . MC JUNIOR
15 JU . STEVEE B . TERRY B . MC JUNIOR

info.0101 5025499 office.01255 220819 tribe records.01376 325228 the barn
when.each and every friday night 8 till late
where.the essex barn, rayne road, braintree
TRIBE RECORDS IN CLACTON IS OPEN AT 40-42 HIGH ST. CLACTON TEL 01255 220819

£6 entrance
over 21's only
r.o.a.r. come early!

novFLY.95b

deep inside

design Eg.G

nov dec
24 STEVEE B . RAY HURLEY(bass) . RUSS . MC JUNIOR
01 JAMIE SMART(wanted records) . TERRY B . STEVEE B . BRIAN T(ginger beer)

info.0101 5025499 office.01255 220819 tribe records
when.each and every friday night 8 till late
where.the essex barn, rayne road, braintree
barn t.01376 325228

£6 entrance
over 21's only
r.o.a.r. come early!

Eg.G; Deep Inside
@ [The Essex Barn], Braintree;
Nov/Dec 1995

deep inside

£6 entrance
over 21's only
r.o.a.r. come early!

info.0101 5025499 office.01255 220819 tribe records.01376 325228 the barn
when.each and every friday night 8 till late
where.the essex barn, rayne road, braintree
TRIBE RECORDS IN CLACTON IS OPEN AT 40-42 HIGH ST. CLACTON TEL 01255 220819

nov
10 JU . STEVEE B . TERRY B . MC JUNIOR
17 STEVEE B . TERRY B . JU . TERRY G

Eg.G; Deep Inside @ [The Essex Barn], Braintree; Dec 1995

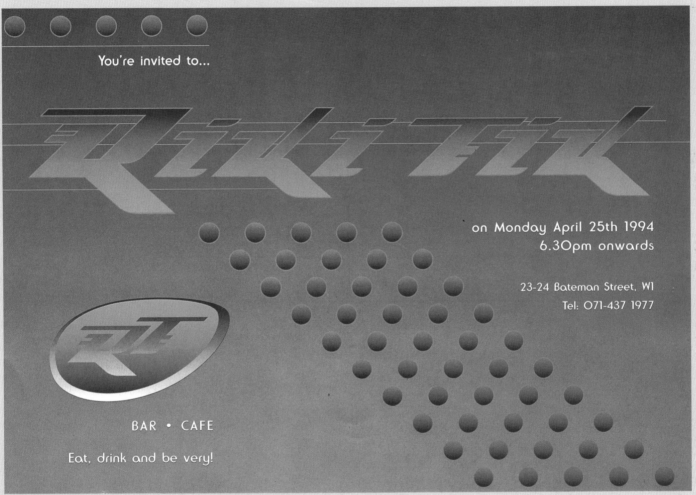

ME Company; [Riki-Tiks], London; April 1994

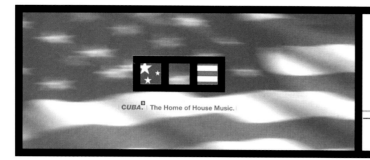
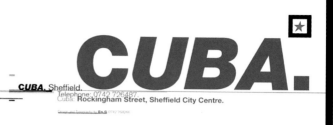

Eg.G; [Cuba], Sheffield; Nov 1993

P.C. @ The Haçienda;
Domina @ [The Haçienda], Manchester; July 1995

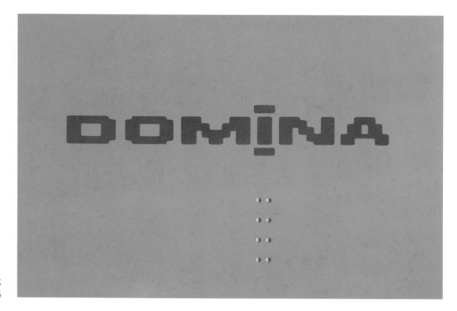

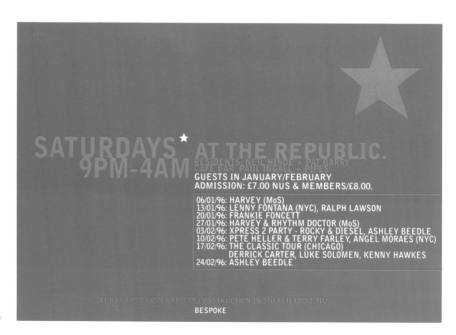

Designers Republic; [The Republic], Sheffield;
Jan/Feb 1996

> **"**
> *I rarely produce visuals.*
> I prefer to use the screen
> ## AS A BLANK PIECE
> ## OF CANVAS
> *working and changing things*
> *as I go along.*
>
> **You could say I'm impatient or lazy**
>
> but I find this method goes with
> the nature of the job I have here
> ## @ THE HACIENDA.
>
> TURN ON – PUT DOWN – BUREAU OUT !
> **"**

(P.C. (Paul Cummings))

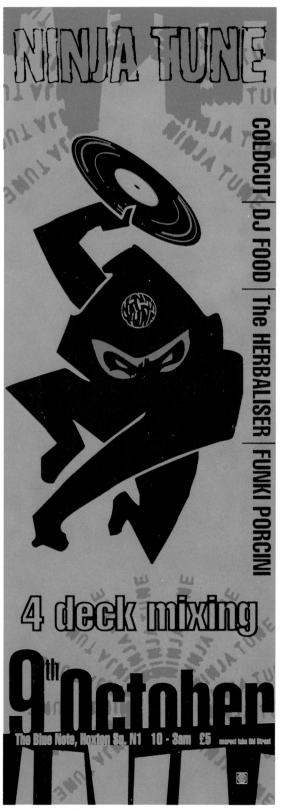

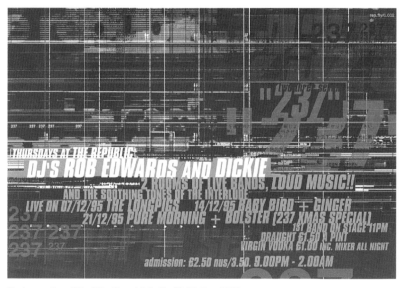

Designers Republic; [The Republic], Sheffield; Dec 1995

Kevin Foakes @ Openmind; Ninja Tune @ [The Blue Note], London; Oct 1995

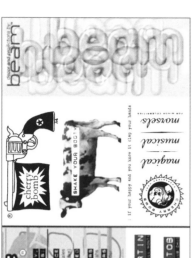

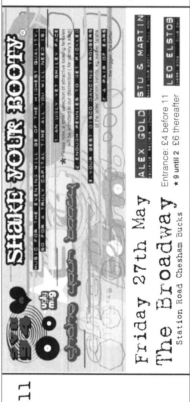

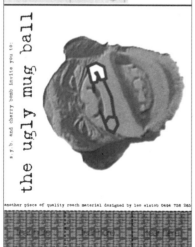

> Just as I love to hear Jazz
> next to Techno or Disco or Dub Reggae –
> in a musical collage, I love the idea of **mixing**
> **old TV sets, Indian drawings, graffiti tags**
> and Macintosh doodles
> together to form one visually.

(Leo Elstob)

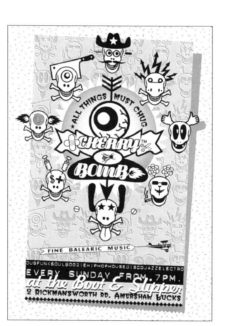

Leo Elstob – Bushfire Design; Cherry Bomb @
[The Boot and Slipper], Amersham;
Sundays 1994

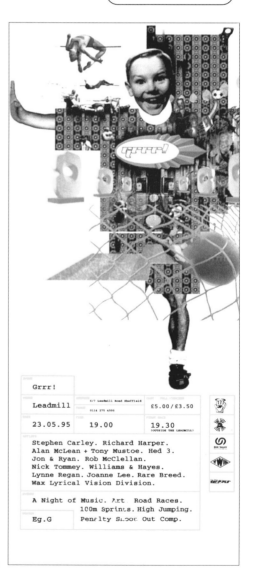

Eg.G; Grrr! @ the [Leadmill], Sheffield; May 1995

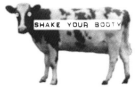
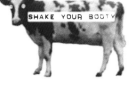

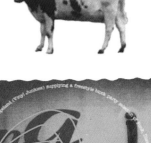

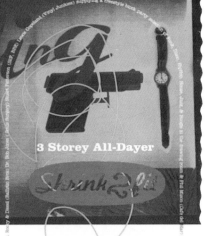

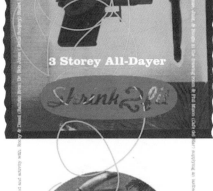

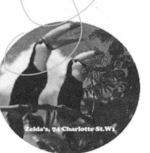

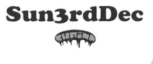

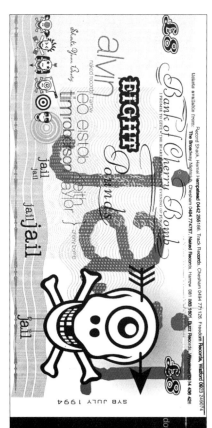

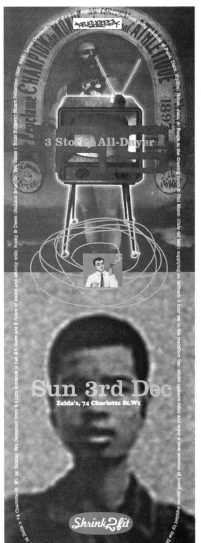

Leo Elstob – Bushfire Design; Shrink 2 Fit @ [Zelda's], London; Dec 1995

Leo Elstob – Bushfire Design; Shrink 2 Fit @ [Zelda's], London; Dec 1995

Leo Elstob – Bushfire Design; Shake Your Booty @ [The Broadway], Chesham; July 1994

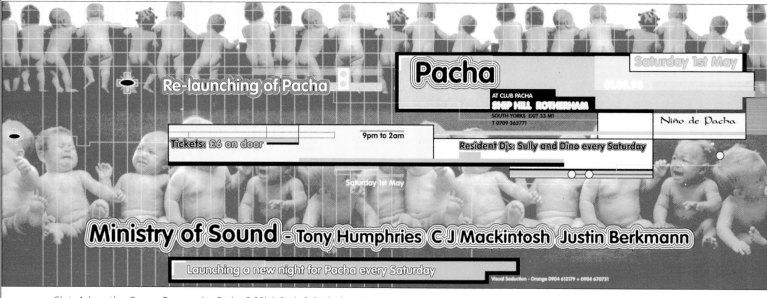

Chris Ashworth – Orange Typography; Pacha @ [Club Pacha], Rotherham; May 1995

Chris Ashworth – Orange Typography; Ask Yer Dad @ [Venus], Nottingham; Oct 1992

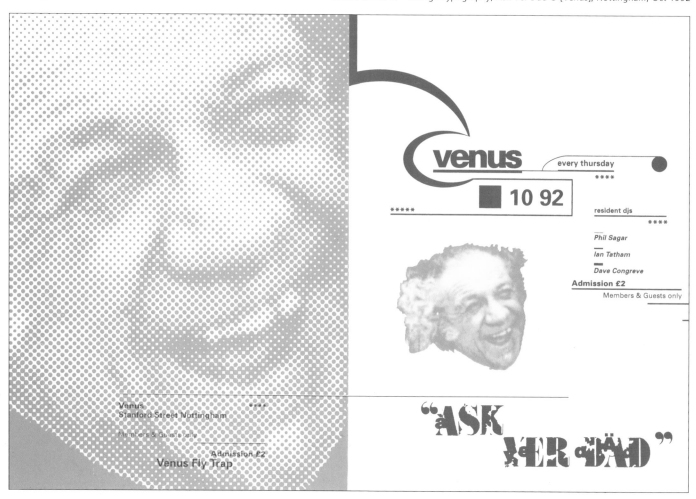

Chris Ashworth – Orange Typography; Odyssey @ [Toffs
Nightclub], York; June 1992

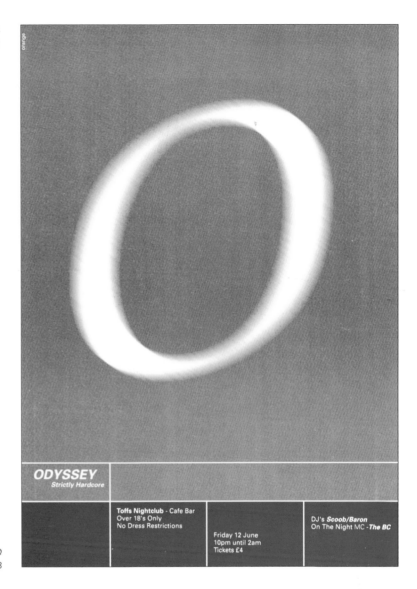

ODYSSEY
Strictly Hardcore

Toffs Nightclub - Cafe Bar
Over 18's Only
No Dress Restrictions

Friday 12 June
10pm until 2am
Tickets £4

DJ's *Scoob/Baron*
On The Night MC - *The BC*

Chris Ashworth – Orange Typography; Lose Your Furniture @
[Venus], Nottingham; Feb 1993

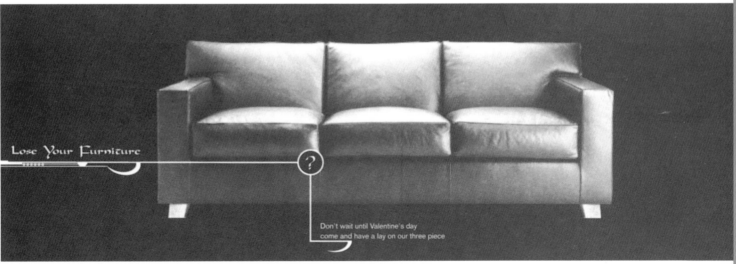

Lose Your Furniture

?

Don't wait until Valentine's day
come and have a lay on our three piece

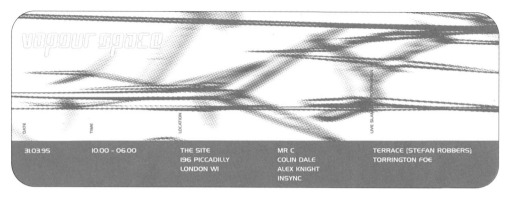

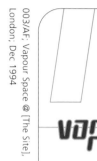

DATE	TIME	LOCATION		LIVE SLAMMIN
31.03.95	10.00 - 06.00	THE SITE 196 PICCADILLY LONDON W1	MR C COLIN DALE ALEX KNIGHT INSYNC	TERRACE [STEFAN ROBBERS] TORRINGTON FOE

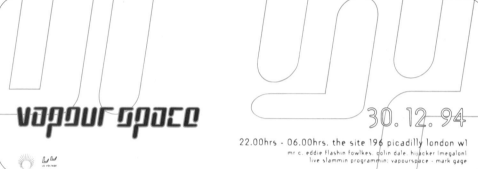

vapour space

30. 12. 94

22.00hrs - 06.00hrs. the site 196 picadilly london w1

mr c. eddie flashin fowlkes. colin dale. hijacker [megalon]
live slammin programmin: vapourspace - mark gage

LV LO VOLTAGE

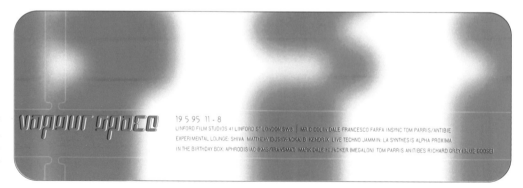

vapour space

19 5 95 11 - 8

LINFORD FILM STUDIOS 41 LINFORD ST LONDON SW8 | MR C COLIN DALE FRANCESCO FARFA INSYNC TOM PARRIS/ANTIBIE

EXPERIMENTAL LOUNGE: SHIVA MATTHEW [BUSHWADKA] B. KENDRIX LIVE TECHNO JAMMIN: LA SYNTHESIS ALPHA PROXIMA

IN THE BIRTHDAY BOX: APHRODISIAC [KMS/TRANSMAT] MARK DALE HIJACKER [MEGALON] TOM PARRIS ANITIBES RICHARD GREY [BLUE GOOSE]

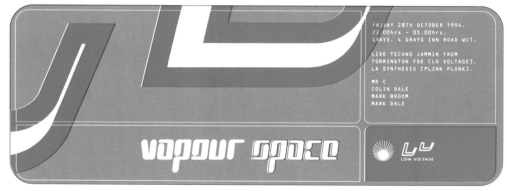

FRIDAY 28TH OCTOBER 1994.
22.00hrs - 05.00hrs.
GRAYS, 4 GRAYS INN ROAD WC1.

LIVE TECHNO JAMMIN FROM
TORRINGTON FOE [LO VOLTAGE].
LA SYNTHESIS [PLINK PLONK].

MR C
COLIN DALE
MARK BROOM
MARK DALE

vapour space

LV
LOW VOLTAGE

003/AF; Vapour Space @ [The Site], London; Feb 1995

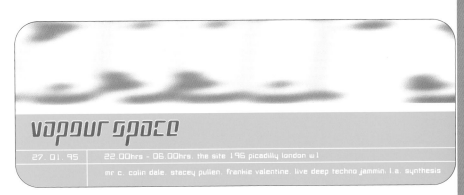

003/AF; Vapour Space @ [The Site], London; Jan 1995

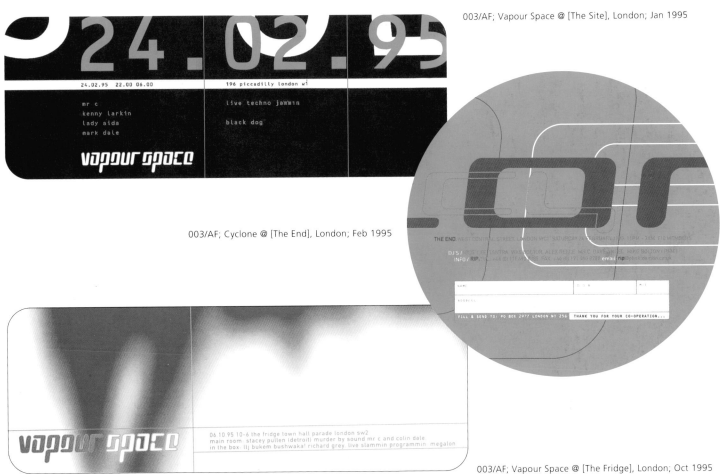

003/AF; Cyclone @ [The End], London; Feb 1995

003/AF; Vapour Space @ [The Fridge], London; Oct 1995

003/AF; Vapour Space @ [The Fridge], London; Dec 1995

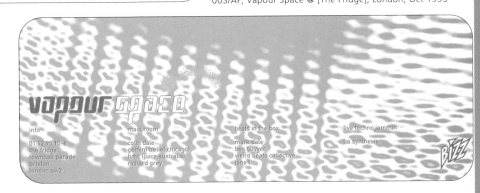

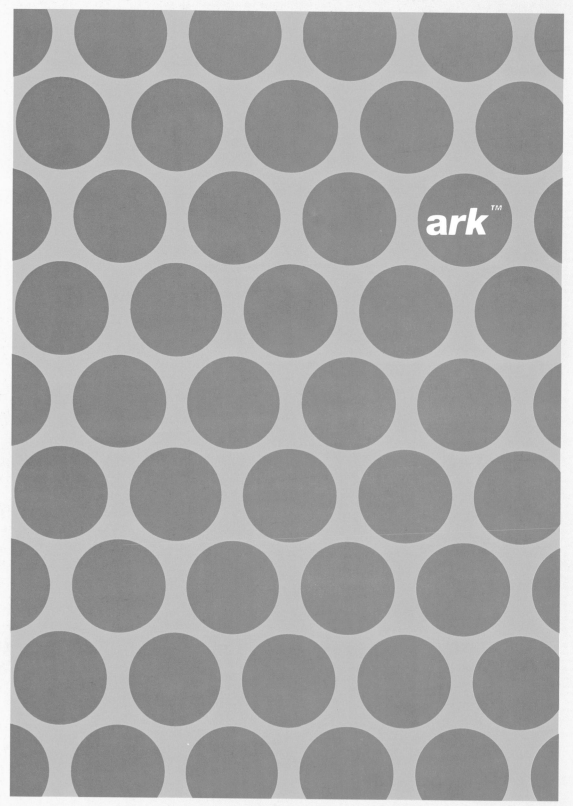

Rob Tyrrel @ Ark; Ark/Exposure present Ark @ [The Palais], Sheffield; April 1992

Patrick Eugene Murphy @ Design Definition; Bedlam @ [The Empress Rooms], Mexborough; March 1992

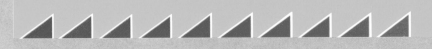
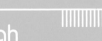

DESIGN DEFINITION
0226 297694

Bedlam
7th March

The EMPRESS Rooms

Swinton Road, Mexborough

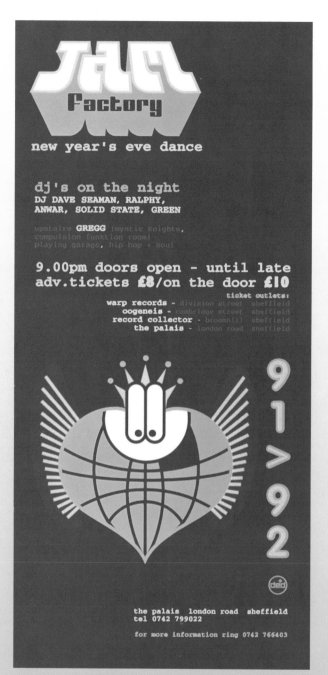

DED Associates; Jam Factory @ [The Palais], Sheffield;
New Years Eve 1991

DED Associates; Peace @ [Kiki's], Sheffield; May 1992

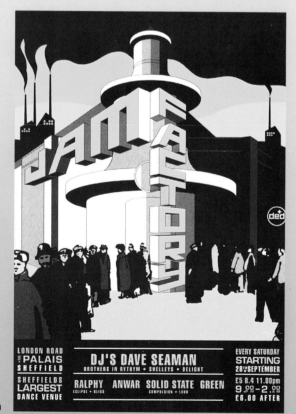

DED Associates; Jam Factory @ [The Palais], Sheffield; Sept 1990

Vague

penetrates deep into all areas

SUPERMIXED

Vague

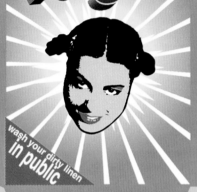

wash your dirty linen **in public**

WARNING Don't bother coming if you're homophobic, looking for a freakshow or easily offended

SUPERMIXED

Vague

INSTRUCTIONS

vague is and always has been a mixed club for gay, lesbian and bisexual people, single women, cross dressers, transvestites, transexuals and misfits.
vague aims to provide a safe space that is dedicated to greater inter-racial and inter-sexual understanding.

We consistently work with local AIDS groups and charities in order to increase safe sex awareness.

wash your dirty linen in public at vague

colorsafe
CONTAINS AGROTEC

tested and recommended

penetrates deep into all areas

Vague

Paul Fryer @ Mongrel Graphics; Supermixed
Vague @ [The Warehouse], Leeds; 1994

Paul Fryer @ Mongrel Graphics; Hi Power Vague
@ [The Warehouse], Leeds; 1994

❊ **VAGUE** ❊
HI POWER

VAGUE
HI POWER

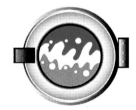

CLEAN UP YOUR ACT

WITH ADDED TWA
CAUTION: irritants

VAGUE HI POWER

surfing the information super alleyway

VAGUE
ACTIONS SPEAK LOUDER THAN WE DO

What a pair of TWAts

at the **cutting edge** of an evolutionary **dead end**

A right load of bollocks gets talked about vague, so let's dispel a few myhths:

' Vague has no dress code; Suitability is decided on your attitude.

' Vague is not a straight or gay club; it is a MIXED club.

' Vague is for broadminded and progressive individuals; we don't want bigots whatever their sexual preference may be.

' Vague is not concerned with fads or fashion; we don't do things coz they're cool or trendy; we are interested in EVOLUTION and INTEGRATION.

IF YOU LIKE THESE IDEAS, YOU ARE WELCOME AT OUR CLUB

VAGUE WITH ADDED TWA
HI POWER   CAUTION: irritants ❊

VAGUE ❊
HI POWER

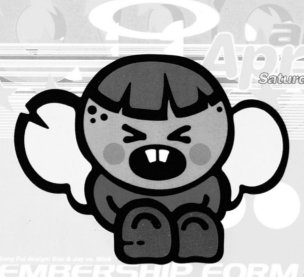

April 94

Saturdays.02nd Pa by **HYPER GO GO**
(High, Never Let Go, Raise)*

09th **WELLY & MATT BELL**

16th **RETRO.** Pa by **MANIC**
(I'm Coming Hardcore)...a night of club classics*

23rd **CARL COX** Plays House

30th Pa by **TC 91.92.93.94**
Direct from Italy (Berry, Harmony, Funky Guitar)*

Angels resident dj's are: Paul Taylor, Fresh & Rick B
Admission: £6 members. £8 non members *Admission £7 members, £9 non members
Angels. PO Box 68 Curzon Street, Burnley, Lancashire BB11 1BX. M65 exit junction 10, in town
centre (next to M&S) tel: 0282 35222 / 0836 544661. Over 18's only - ID required - Dress code

Membership is free. Send this slip to us, enclosing a S.A.E. for guaranteed reduced admission. Are you interested
in organising a coach party from your area at reduced rates ? If so, give us a call and we will organise it for you

MEMBERSHIP FORM
name   d.o.b
address / postcode

Hong Kong Fui design: Gav & Jay vs. Wink

Wink Associates; [Angels], Burnley; April 1994

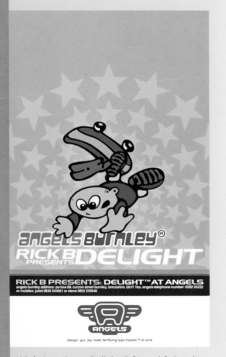

Wink Associates; Delight @ [Angels], Burnley;
Oct 1994

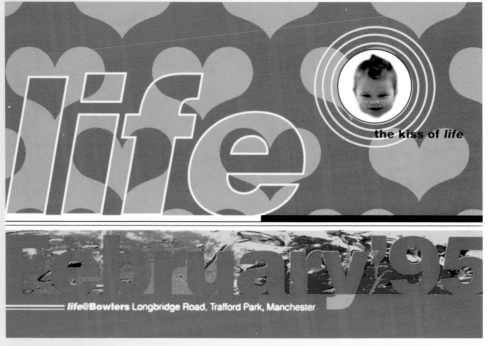

Jason O'Connor @ The Life Organisation; The Kiss of Life @ [Bowlers], Manchester; Feb 1995

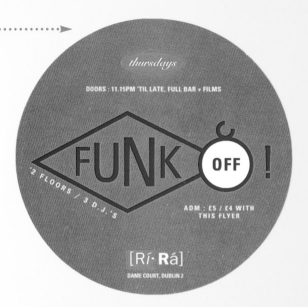

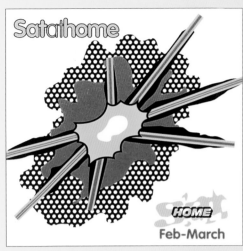

David Marsh and Peter Tunstall @ Tangent Design;
Sat at Home @ [Home], Manchester; Feb/March 1995

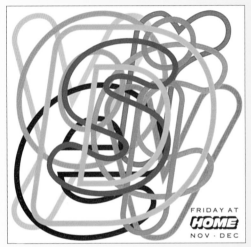

David Marsh and Peter Tunstall @ Tangent Design;
Discovery @ [Home], Manchester; Nov/Dec 1994

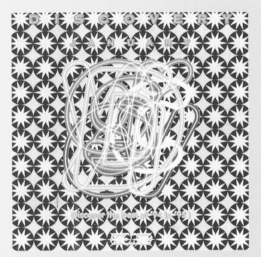

David Marsh and Peter Tunstall @ Tangent Design;
Discovery @ [Home], Manchester; Jan 1995

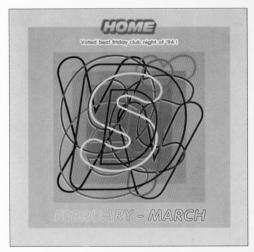

David Marsh and Peter Tunstall @ Tangent Design;
Discovery @ [Home], Manchester; Feb/March 1994

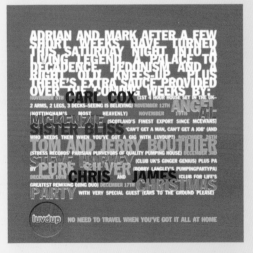

David Marsh and Peter Tunstall @ Tangent Design;
Sat at Home @ [Home], Manchester; Nov/Dec 1994

Danny Jenkins – FAB 4; Solid State @ [Lakota], Bristol; May 1995

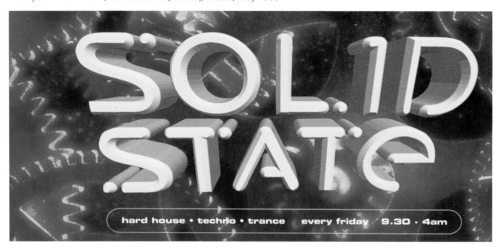

hard house • techno • trance   every friday   9.30 - 4am

Chris Childs – The Strutt Club;
Strutt @ [The Cross], London; Nov/Dec 1994

" It appeals to, and targets, a like-minded,
electronic-music-loving person! "

Chris Childs

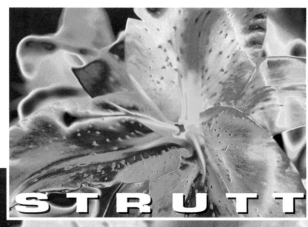

STRUTT

Wink Associates; Fate @ [Republica], Manchester; Nov 1995

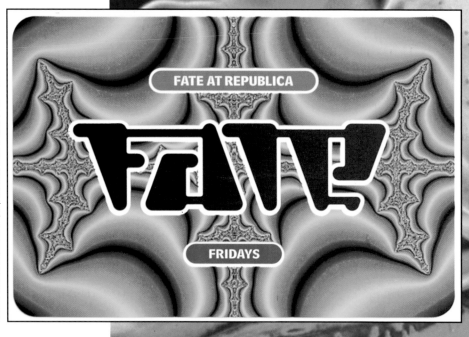

FATE AT REPUBLICA

FATE

FRIDAYS

The Haçienda & Attitude present

FLESH

Craig Johnson; Flesh @ [The Haçienda], Manchester; Oct 1991

Chris Childs – The Strutt Club; Strutt @ [Grays], London; June/July 1994

"Club flyers should be ephemeral and disposable. However, it's debatable that mere paper and ink can continue to reflect the cutting edge of clubland's creativity and technology."

(Pete Riley)

As an art, flyer design is unique, fun and rewarding. As an occupation it's inadvisable. "

(Pete Riley)

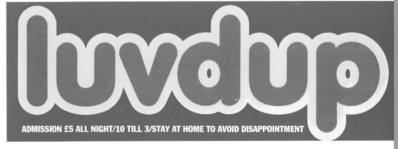

ADMISSION £5 ALL NIGHT/10 TILL 3/STAY AT HOME TO AVOID DISAPPOINTMENT

Pete Riley (Logo Design Graham Tunna); Luvdup @ [Home], Manchester; Feb 1995

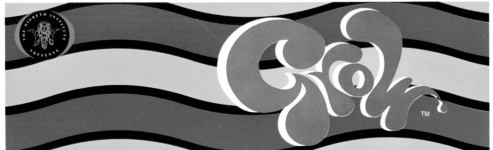

Emelle Creative; Grow @ [The Digbeth Institute], Birmingham; Feb 1995

Graham Newman; Fac51 The Haçienda and Renaissance meet
@ the [Ministry of Sound], London; March 1993; July 1993

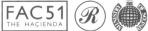

5th March

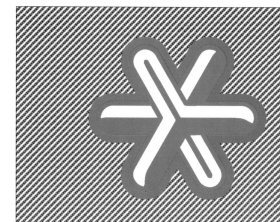

2nd July

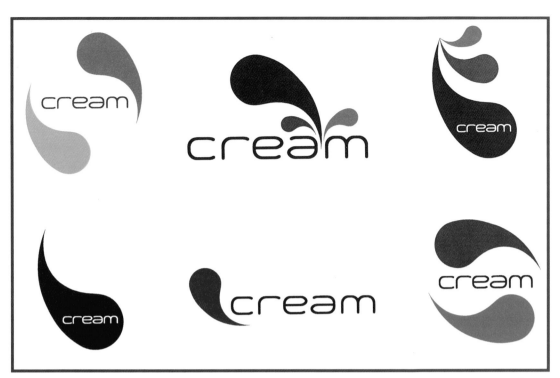

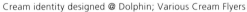

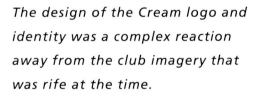

Cream identity designed @ Dolphin; Various Cream Flyers

The design of the Cream logo and identity was a complex reaction away from the club imagery that was rife at the time.

At the time the logo was designed (Summer 1994), Cream was an ambitious club that had plans to expand. Therefore it was important to the club that they needed to be branded, the logo would have to be recognisable and strong enough to be used on ads, flyers, club projections and merchandise. Since 1994 Cream has gone on to become the biggest and most successful club in Britain.

Rob Petrie @ Dolphin

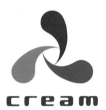

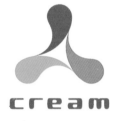

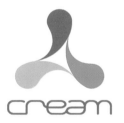

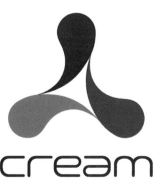

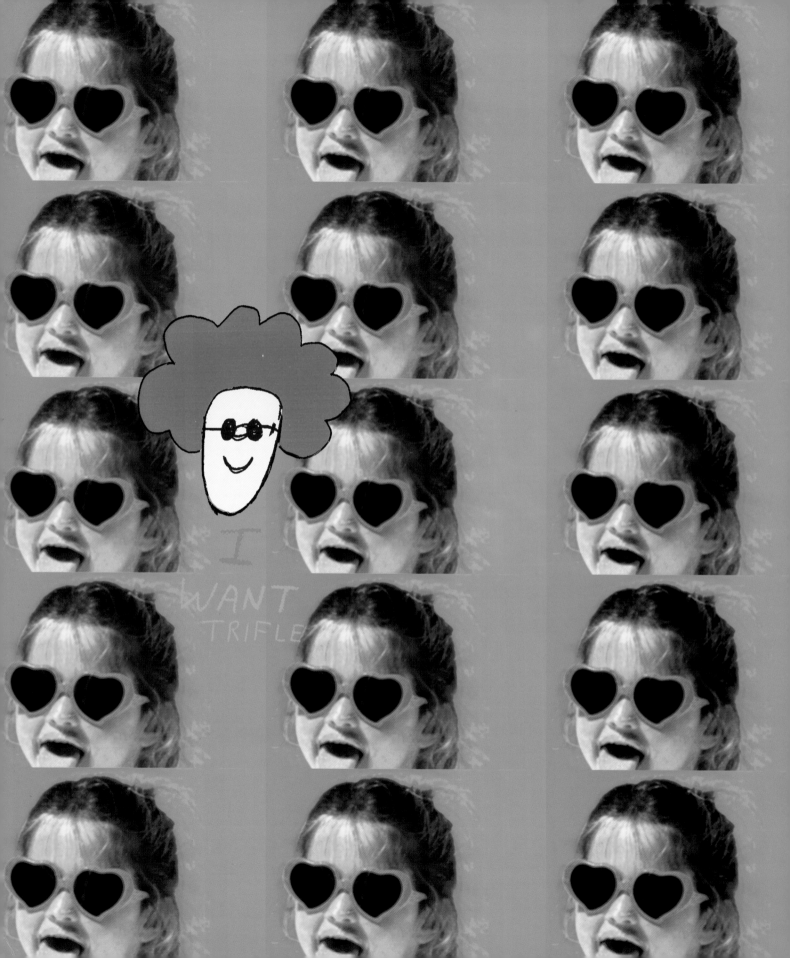

Theme	**affirmed**	– frivolity
Presenting the	**animated**	inanimates – the reality dreamers of
Confections mixed by 'Sponge Cake' to intrigue + entice you		DE DEJAVU XU JEJAVU
Location	**arranged**	– a neon fairground with space-age cocktail bar
Fuelled by 'Fantasy Enthusiasts'		
	assured	to turn the whites of your eggs red
	Build	a carousel scene
whirling complex custard	**colour**	chic
	Create	castor sugar-plum fairies
with glacé cherries to	**decorate**	
	Discover	random acts of kindness
	dressed	senselessly in frocks
False glitter	**dyed**	eye lashes, feather Goa, Goldie, Cox
	Enter	timelessness.
	Fashion	– watches without hands –
	fry	away time, pantomime; almonds aren't foreverforeverfore !
	Generate	heat•smoke•light•smell•steam
	Hear	
	house –	sound the sprinklers
PREPARE FOR LIFT-OFF	**ignite!!!**	100's + 1000's stargazing, exhilarating love hearts, queen of tarts
Dessert all	**labels**	+ gather your breath for the next ascent
Open your	**mind**	
disclose your	**name**	
	occupy	a space – off again, taking a marathon ride around the room
Mind still	**open ???**	can you survive ? role reversal
	organise	your disguise
A Mud	**pack**	
a	**paper**	chaser, handsome + gentle, lost their way
'there's no	**place**	like home........cookin'
A desire to drive yourself ever onwards and upwards, rotator, rotator ....PAUSE **‖**		
re	**play**	>>>but slower.
re	**run**	
re	**stop**	
re	**turn**	
re	**use**	
re	**wind**	

DRAWN INWARD

why? "FOR GENTLE OVERNIGHT RELIEF!"

EAT TRIFLE NOT BEEF

X X X

Steve Williams

> *Flyers are the modern football cards of today's playground.*
>
> Taragh Bissett

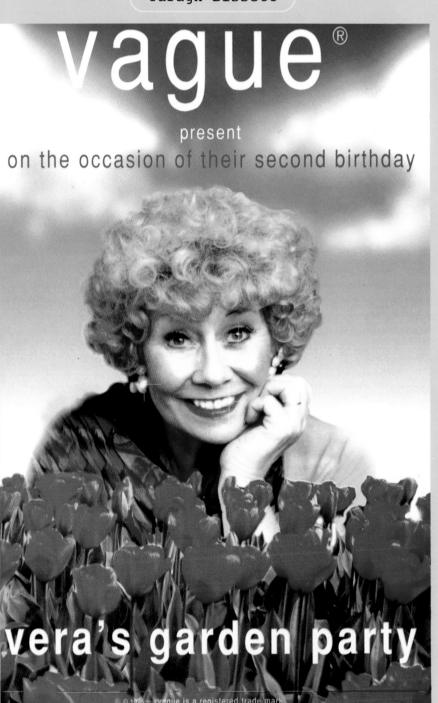

Paul Fryer @ Mongrel Graphics; Vague present Vera's Garden Party @ [The Warehouse], Leeds; July 1995

Jonathan Cutting; Glitterati @ [The Cross], London; Jan 1996

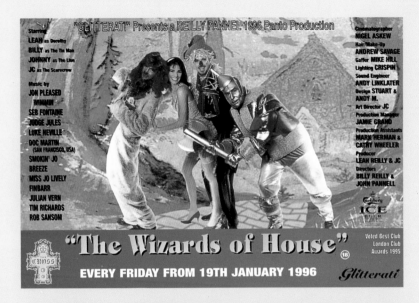

Paul Fryer @ Mongrel Graphics; Vague @ [Hiflyers],
Leeds; April 1993

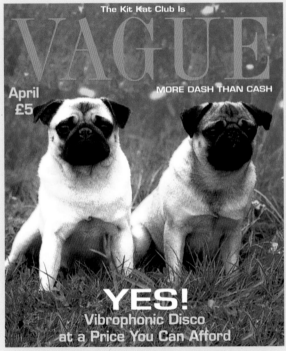

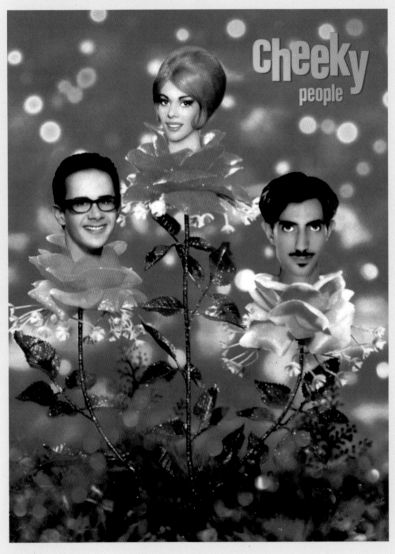

Andrew Graham; Cheeky People @ [The Cross], London, June 1995

Leisure Lounge

Kjeld Van Schreven; [Leisure Lounge], London; April 1995

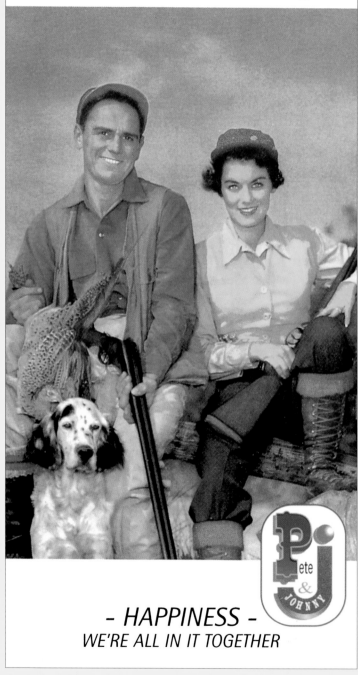

Leisure Lounge

- HAPPINESS -
WE'RE ALL IN IT TOGETHER

Kjeld Van Schreven; [Leisure Lounge], London; March 1995

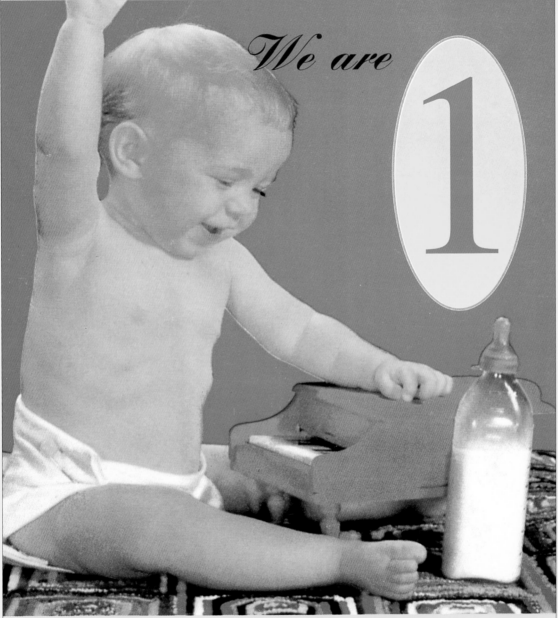

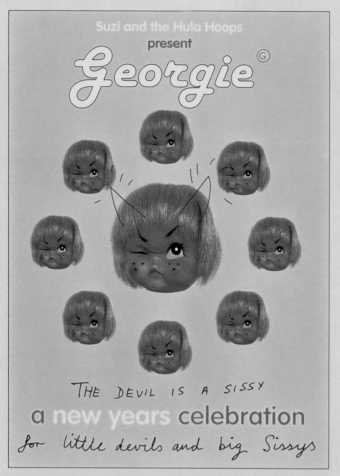

Craig Richards; Georgie @ a secret location, London; New Years Eve 1995

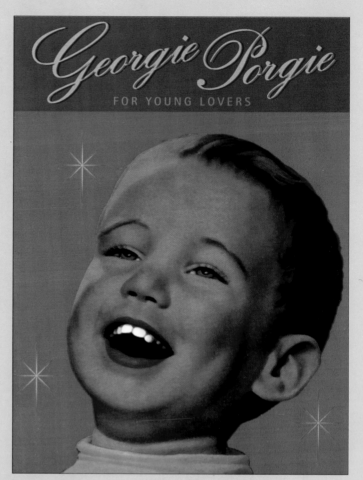

Craig Richards; Georgie @ a secret location, London; New Years Eve 1993

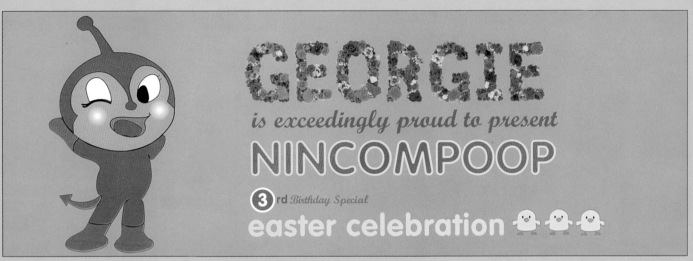

Craig Richards; Georgie @ a secret location, London; April 1996

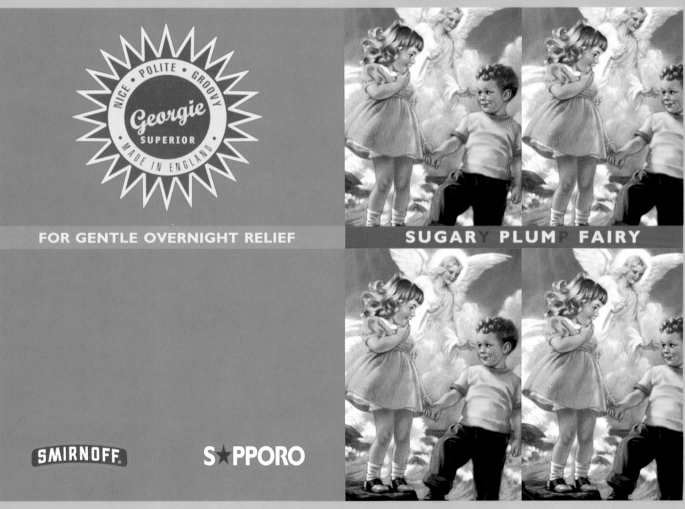

Craig Richards; Georgie @ a secret location, London; New Years Eve 1994

Naked Design; I-Spy @ Leeds Metropolitan University (Poly); Feb 1993

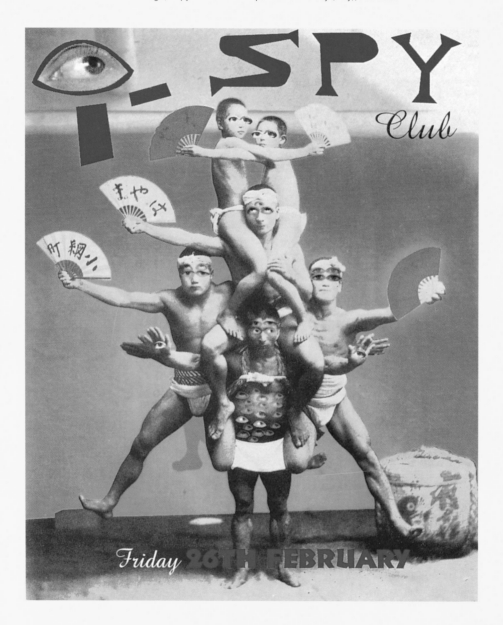

Craig Richards;
Malibu Stacey
@ [Hanover Grand],
London; July 1995

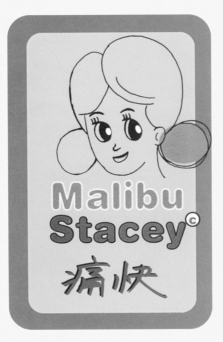

Craig Richards;
Malibu Stacey
@ [Hanover Grand],
London; July 1994

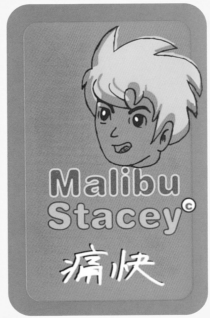

Craig Richards;
Malibu Stacey
@ [Hanover Grand],
London; Feb/March 1995.
(Inside and front)

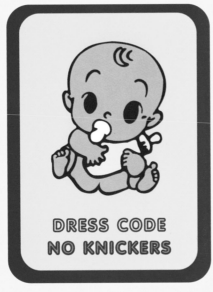

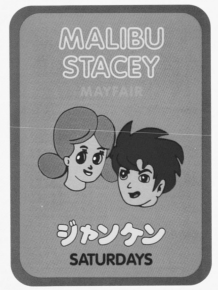

Craig Richards; Georgie. This was intended to be the first Georgie party. Cancelled due to legal reasons.

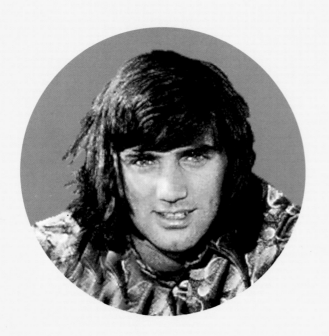

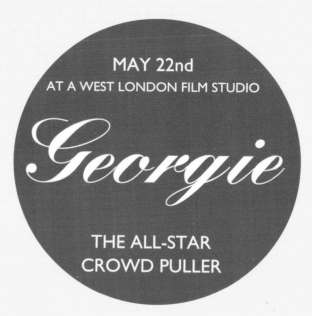

MAY 22nd
AT A WEST LONDON FILM STUDIO

Georgie

THE ALL-STAR
CROWD PULLER

Ian Whittaker; Wildlife
@ [Mountford Hall],
Liverpool University

"

Our flyers are aimed at showing

our punters that we don't take

ourselves too seriously.

Too many flyers are covered with

images of gorgeous women in

tight T-shirts with the club logo,

we're not about that.

Wildlife is about having fun and

the bright and colourful images

on our flyers reflect that.

"

Chris Salmon

Ian Whittaker; Wildlife
@ [Mountford Hall],
Liverpool University;
Feb/March 1994

Ian Whittaker; Wildlife @
[Mountford Hall],
Liverpool University

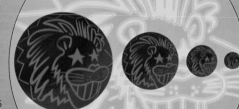

Ian Whittaker; Wildlife
@ [Mountford Hall],
Liverpool University;
April/May/June 1995

WILDLIFE...

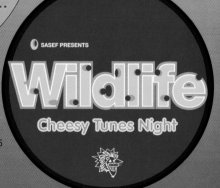

SASEF PRESENTS

Wildlife
Cheesy Tunes Night

Ian Whittaker;
Wildlife
@ [Mountford Hall],
Liverpool University;
March 1996

> **_Ownership_**
>   don't exist,
>   **_authorship_**'s dead
> **DON'T QUOTE**
>   **– STEAL.**

(Knopov)

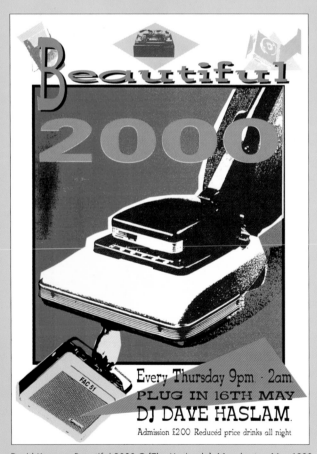

David Knopov; Beautiful 2000 @ [The Haçienda], Manchester; May 1990

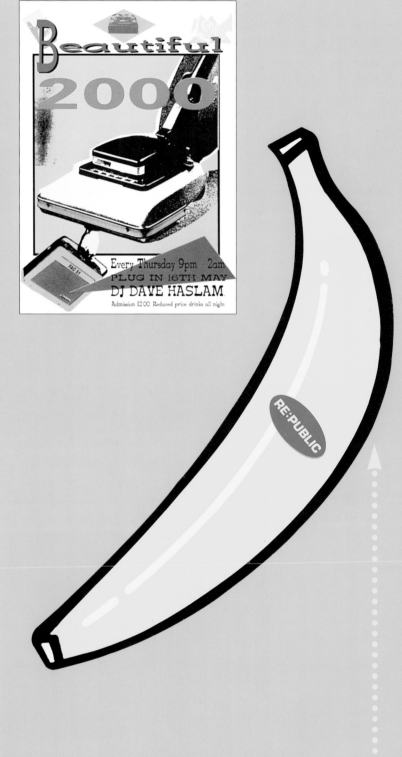

Pete Riley; RE:Public @ [No.1 Club], Manchester; Summer 1993

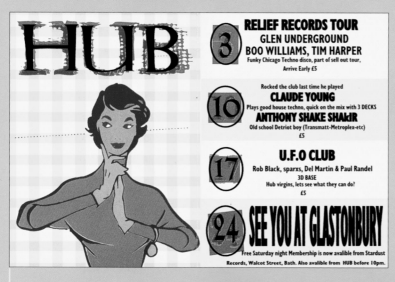

Paddy Malone; [Hub Club], Bath; June 1995

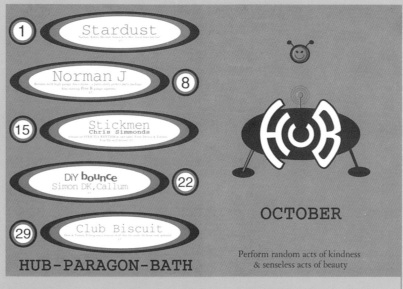

Paddy Malone; [Hub Club], Bath; Oct 1994

Paddy Malone; [Hub Club], Bath; Jan 1995

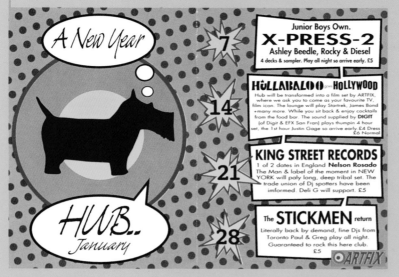

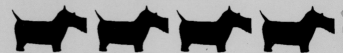

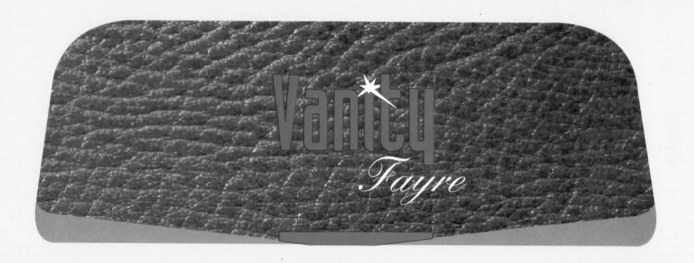

August

5th K Klass Pete Heller Rob Sykes Miss Barbie.   Boudoir Bar Phil Mison Ben & Andy

12th Boy George Fat Tony Luke Neville Mark Felton.Boudoir Bar Marky P Little Andy

19th Mark Moore Craig Jensen Miss Barbie Joe Fish. Boudoir Bar Ben & Andy   Von

26th Fat Tony Craig Jensen Rob Sykes Paul Harris. Boudoir Bar Marky P Jonny Rocca

10.30 pm–5am £12

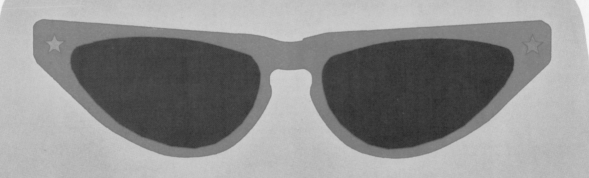

Design Simon & Russell

Russell Hall & Simon Chalmers; Vanity Fayre @ [Raw], London; Aug 1995

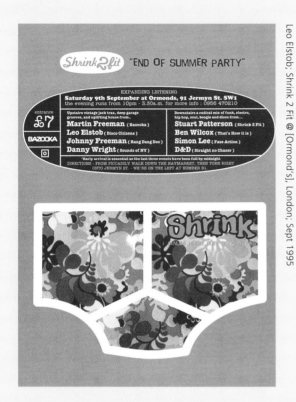

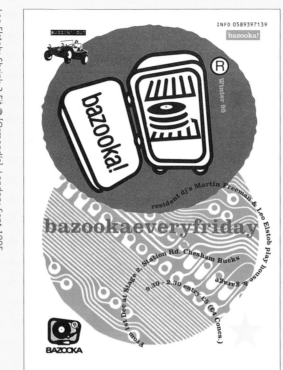

Leo Elstob; Shrink 2 Fit @ [Ormond's], London; Sept 1995

Leo Elstob; Bazooka @ [Stage 2], Chesham; Dec 1995

Leo Elstob; Bazooka @ [The Boot and Slipper], Amersham; Summer 1995

Leo Elstob; Bazooka @ [The Broadway], Chesham; Feb 1995

Leo Elstob; (detail of) Bazooka Bites Back @ Stage 2, Chesham; Feb 1996

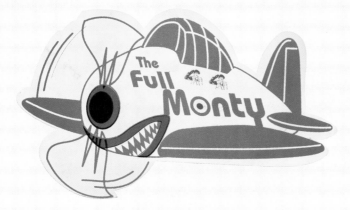

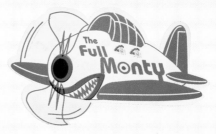

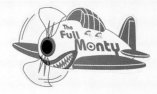

Mark Barclay;
The Full Monty @ [Mirage],
Windsor; Jan 1994

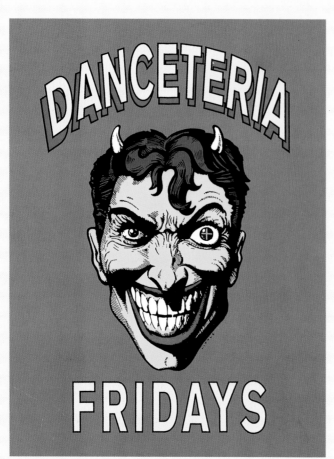

DANCETERIA

FRIDAYS

Dave Little; Danceteria @ the [Limelight], London; 1992

Danny Jenkins; Brave @ [Lakota], Bristol; Jan 1993

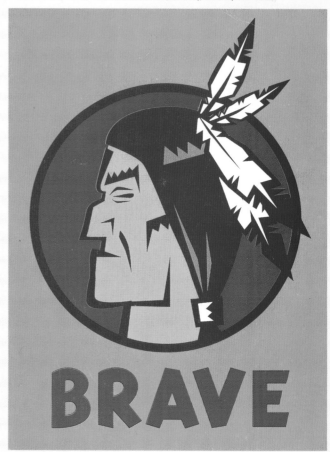

BRAVE

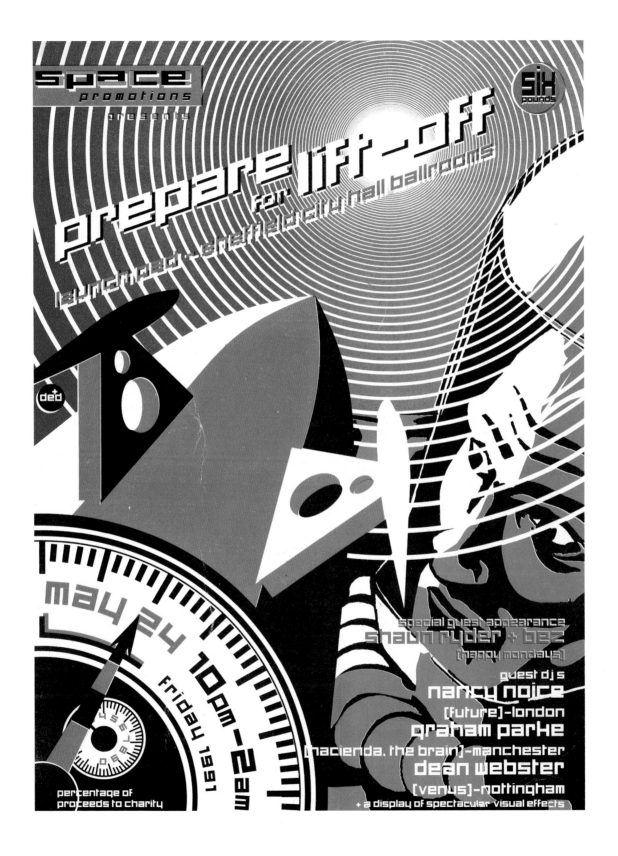

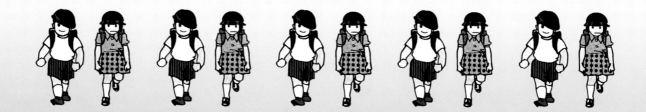

> ## "
> FLYERS WERE MY ROUTE INTO GRAPHIC DESIGN; RUNNING THE
> CLUBS MYSELF MEANT I HAD A VERY REASONABLE CLIENT TO
> NEGOTIATE WITH, ALTHOUGH HE PAYS VERY BADLY.
> "

(Fred Deakin)

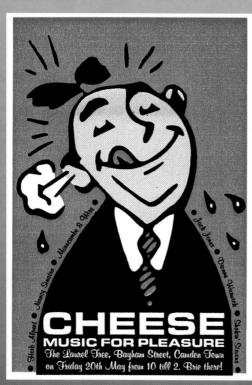

Fred Deakin; Cheese @ [The Laurel Tree], London;
May 1994

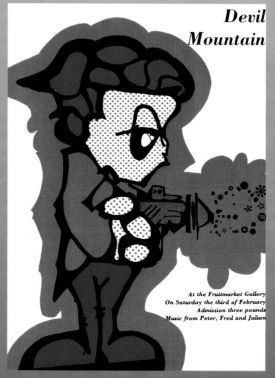

Fred Deakin; Devil Mountain @ [The Fruitmarket Gallery],
Edinburgh; Feb 1990

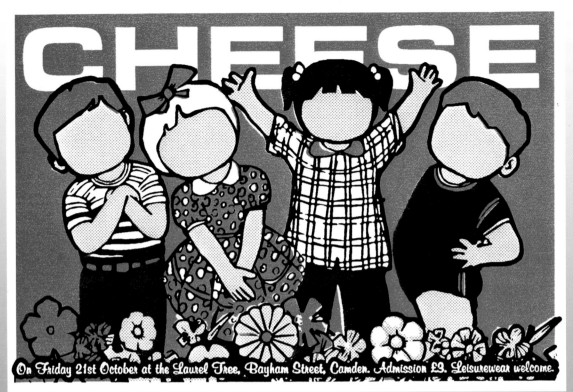

Fred Deakin; Cheese @ [The Laurel Tree], London; Oct 1994

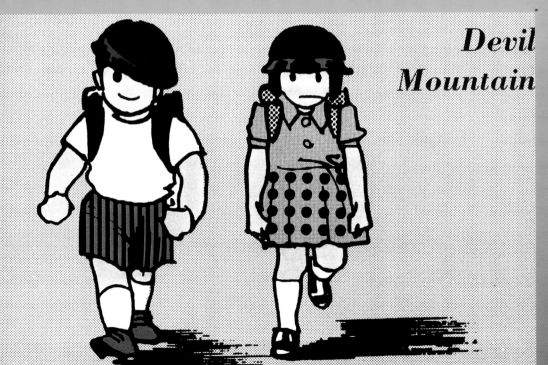

Fred Deakin; Devil Mountain @ [The Fruitmarket Gallery], Edinburgh; Feb 1990

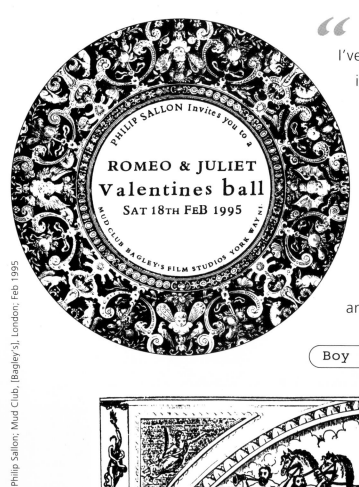

I've seen Ms Philip agonising over her invites –
it's a labour of love to the point of exhaustion.
By the way, she doesn't call them flyers,

they're invitations,

and she doesn't hand them out outside clubs –
she does it inside by herself from a plastic
Tesco's carrier bag

and then she gets thrown out!

Boy George on Philip Sallon

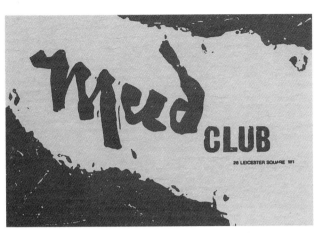

Philip Sallon; Mud Club @ 28 Leicester Square, London; 1983
(First Mud Flyer)

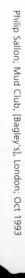

Philip Sallon; Mud Club, [Bagley's], London; Oct 1994

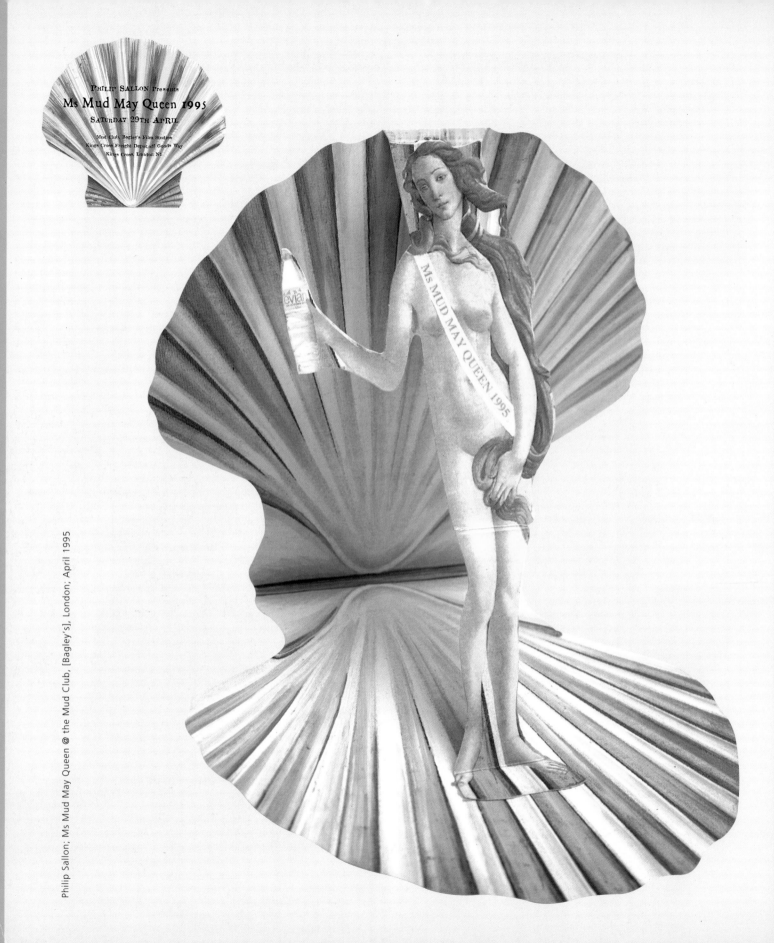

Philip Sallon; Ms Mud May Queen @ the Mud Club, [Bagley's], London; April 1995

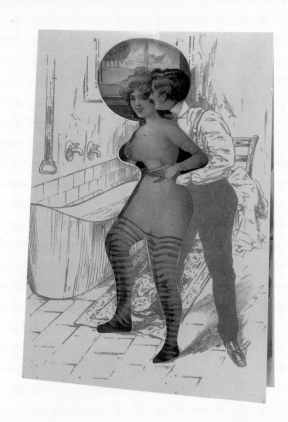

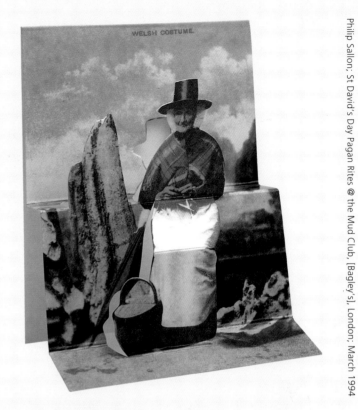

WELSH COSTUME.

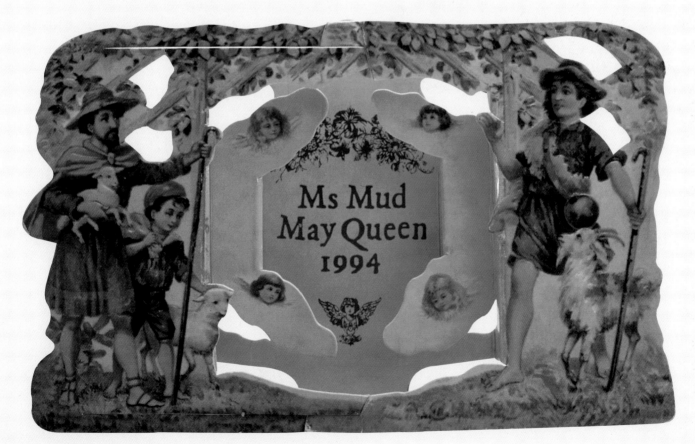

Ms Mud
May Queen
1994

Philip Sallon; Ms Mud May Queen @ the Mud Club, [Bagley's], London; April 1994

The Pussy Posse Presents...
PAMELA PAMPER

On Sunday 26th April   7.00 pm Prompt

"There's nothing Pamela enjoys more than a full steam and massage with her friends; especially when her favorite tunes are playing.

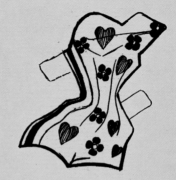

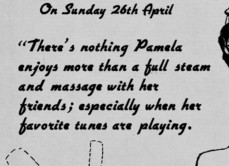

Her nails always need manicuring and her lovely locks dressed; because Pamela works her fingers to the bone and can often be seen dragged through a bush backwards. But when she's not snogging her favorite 'boys' in town, she loves to relax, stuff her face, feel it go pink in the heat, and appreciate herself."

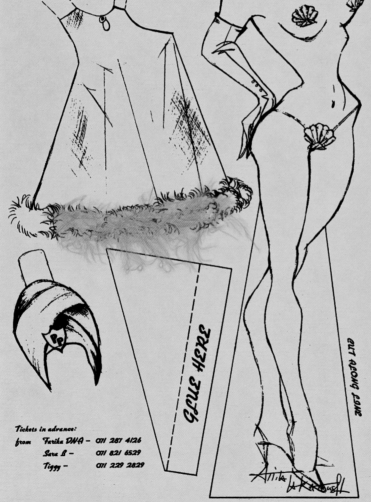

GLUE HERE

CUT ALONG LINE

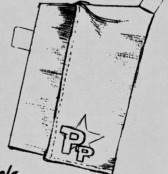

Tickets in advance:
from   Farika DNA –   071 287 4126
        Sara B –   071 821 6529
        Tiggy –   071 229 2829

Come Pamper Yourself with Pamela

At: The Porchester Spa, Porchester Road, W2   Dress Bare as you Dare   Birds Only

Susan puts on
her blue party dress
for the Mud club
1st Birthday party.

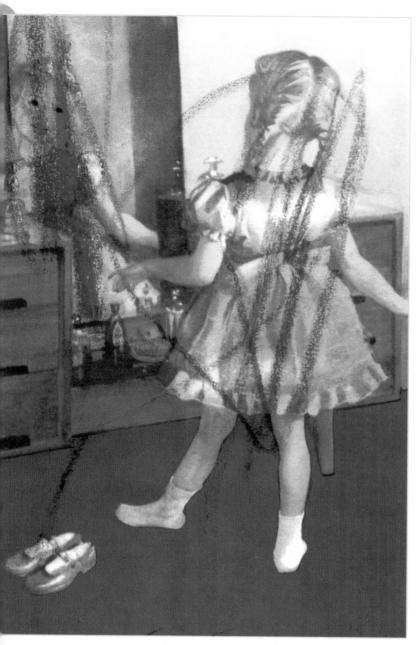

Philip Sallon; Mud Club 1st Birthday @ [Bagley's], London; Aug 1994

ARTISTS' ADDRESSES

Nicola Ackland-Snow
3 The Avenue
Moordown
Bournemouth

Chris Ashworth @ Substance
139c Underhill Road
London SE22

Mark Barclay
Unit 26
The Village
High Street
Slough

Billion Dollar Babes
23a Landill Road
London W9

Taragh Bissett
Greenways
South Hill Avenue
London HA1

Chris Childs
PO Box 7162
London NW6

P.C. (Paul Cummings) @
The Haçienda
11–13 Whitworth Street
West
Manchester

Jonathan Cutting
The Cross
Kings Cross Goods Yard
York Way
London N1

Fred Deakin
Unit 65, Pall Mall Deposit
124–28 Barlby Road
London W10

Danny De Courtelle
72 Railton Road
London SE24

DED Associates
Globe Works
Penistowe Road
Sheffield

Designers Republic
Unit 415
The Workstation
15 Paternoster Row
Sheffield

Dirtbox
NFA

Eg.G
The Workstation
15 Paternoster Row
Sheffield

Leo Elstob @ Bushfire Design
Little Braziers Farm
Belling Don
Chesham

FAB 4
2b St Andrews Road
Montpellier
Bristol

Kevin Foakes @ Openmind
Flat 1, 10 Lyndhurst Way
London SE15

Paul Fryer @ Mongrel
Graphics
Charlie Girl Records Ltd
Lindhurst House
Carlton Road
Livers Edge

George Giorgiou
The Garden Flat
25 Landhill Road
London W9

Gism Productions Limited
2 Warwick Avenue
London HA8

Daniel Gould
26 Fletcher Road
Chigwell
Essex

Andrew Graham
2 Sawkins Close
London SW19

Nick Gundill @ ar:5e Design
Rutland House
38–42 Call Lane
Leeds

Russell Hall/Simon Chalmers
2 Hartham Road
London N7

Tom Hingston/Paul Allen
Unit 2, 78 Liverpool Road
London N10

Craig Johnson
Studio 225, Ducie House
Ducie Street
Manchester

Trevor Johnson
Room 7a
Market Buildings
17 Thomas Street
Manchester

Matthew Kaye
South West Litho
Unit R
The Old Brick Yard
Ashton Keyes,
Swindon

Kettle of Fish
PO Box 1
782 Fulham Road
London SW6

Paul Khera
10 Dulwich Road
London SE24

The KM Partnership
39–41 North Road
London N7

David Knopov
27 Rodney Street
Liverpool

Dave Little
Room 130
Canalot Studios
Kensal Road
London W10

Martin Madigan
25 Queen's Road
Windsor

Paddy Malone
Top Floor
19 Belmont Lansdown
Bath

David Marsh/Peter Tunstall @
Tangent Design
Ducie Street
Manchester

Paul Maybury
29 South Anne Street
Dublin 2

Tom McCallion
Flat 4, 11 Tierney Road
London SW2

ME Company
14 Apollo Studios
Charlton Kings Road
London NW5

Patrick Eugene Murphy @
Design Definition
6 Roger Road
Burton Grange
Barnsley

Naked Design
13–14 Lamberts Arcade
Leeds

Graham Newman
The Bootroom
Sunhouse
2–4 Little Peter Street
Manchester

Jason Nicholls/Gavin Taylor
@ Wink Associates
Sunhouse
2–4 Little Peter Street
Manchester

Jason O'Connor @
The Life Organisation
52 Argyle Street
Birkenhead
Merseyside

Kevin Palmer @ Fitch
Commonwealth House
1 New Oxford Street
London SW1

Uday Patel/Joe Slater @
(003/AF)
Flat 2, 113 Holloway Road
London N7

Rob Petrie @ Dolphin
32 Neal Street
London WC2

Pussy Posse (Sara Blondstein)
The Manor House Cottage
Didmarton, Avon

Raise-A-Head
75 The Circle
Queen Elizabeth Street
London SE1

Ric and Deborah Ramswell @
Pushca
National House
2nd Floor, 60–68 Wardour
Street
London W1

Craig Richards
40–41 Great Western
Studios
The Loft Goods Building
Great Western Road
London W9

Pete Riley
Headway
Inex House
Princess Street
Manchester

Philip Sallon
13 Alma Square
London NW8

Kjeld van Schreven
G. Spot Magazine
Unit D, 25 Copperfield Street
London SE1

Michael Speechley
Ground Floor, 34 Lushington
Road
London NW10

Squarepeg Design
34a Barnsley Road
Wakefield

Swifty Typografix
Unit 65, Pall Mall Deposit
124–28 Barlby Road
London W10

Steve Swindells
344a Old Ford Road
London E3

Ceri Thomas @ Acid Jazz
1 Hoxton Square
London N1

Rob Tyrell @ Ark
Rutland House
Call Lane
Leeds

SPECIAL THANKS TO:

Adam & Emma
Adrian (Luvdup)
Ross Allen @ Dorado
Chris Ashworth
Phil Beddard
Ashley & Simone Beedle
Boy George and Eileen @ More
Protein
John Brenton-Hughes
Nik Calamvokis
Colin 'Laughing Gnome' Callan
Paul Campbell (Danger-Trax)
Danny De Courtelle (Deep Funk)
Crispin
Fred Deakin
Designers Republic
DJon & Kari
Dominic (Babes in Toyland)
Dave Dorrell & Sam
Jon Drape @ The Haçienda
David Ellis (PPQ)
Leo Elstob
Emma @ The Blue Note
Fiona & Massimo @ K.O.F.
Stuart Fraser @ Headway
Paul Fryer (TWA)
George Giorgiou
Hannah & Dr. Atomic
Tom Hingston
Howard
Jason @ Ark
Danny Jenkins & co @ FAB 4
Joe & Uday @ Vapour Space
John Kelly
Levi
Lisa @ Sheffield City Hall
Dave Little
Lottie
Paddy 'Hoe' Malone
Maria @ Raw
Ian Mariott

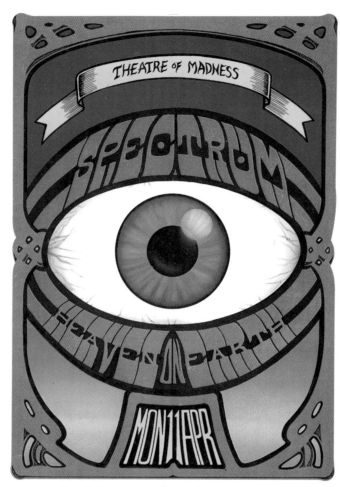

Dave Little; Spectrum @ [Heaven], London; April 1988

Credit to all whose work could not be featured due to lack of space.

Martin & Jane @ The Borderline
Tom McCallion
Sean McClusky & Jim & Tim
Gary Metcalf
Chris Micallef @ Lakota
Mikaela
Colin Morris
Patrick Eugene Murphy & Mum
Richard Newport (Sugar Candy)
Nick @ Leadmill
Richard Oram (Tinstar)
Stuart Patterson
Paul @ Cosies
Paul @ JRM
Peter & Conner @ React
Pussy Posse
Trevor Powell
Quen
Steve Raine @ Hard Times
Raise-A-Head
Jenny & Danny Rampling
Ratty
Sol Ray & Sarah
Leah Reilly
Sav Remzi @ The Blue Note
Craig Richards
Ross @ Concorde
Philip Sallon
Jason Shutt
Stardust
Swifty
Dave Swindells
Tee Pee
Oli Timmins
Toby
Rob Tyrell
Jed Wells
Phil Westoby
Marc Whitman (Musketeer)
Ian Whittaker
Chris Salmon @ Wildlife

Danny Rampling/B Reid; Shoom @
[Busbys], London; Nov 1988